'Absorbing' Gerald Kaufman, *Daily Telegraph*, Books of the Year

'Kelly's use of the film's troubled history of cuts, censorship, [and] banning in every country where it's ever been shown explores cinema's power in society ....' *Premiere*

'Kelly's genuine passion for Milestone's great film is infectious and justified.' David Robinson, *Times Higher Education Supplement*

'The research and the feeling for the film, is the most compelling of any such project I've ever encountered. It recalled such memories that I was tearful when I finished reading it.' Producer Arthur Gardner, who played a German soldier in *All Quiet on the Western Front*

'Here for the first time, is the full story behind the first great masterpiece of the sound cinema ... Kelly's painstaking research has unearthed a wealth of detail, sometimes funny, sometimes moving, but always illuminating. This is a worthy companion to the greatest war movie of all time.' Professor Nicholas Cull, University of Leicester

'This is a superb book, meticulously researched, compulsively readable and consistently fascinating' Professor Jeffrey Richards, Lancaster University

'[*All Quiet on the Western Front*] provides the most detailed documentation on the making of a classic of American cinema ... There is evidence here of considerable and unique research.' Anthony Slide, *Classic Images*

'A concise, thorough and eloquent history of one of the most important – and influential of all American films.' James Curtis, author of *Between Flops: the life of Preston Sturges* and *New World of Gods and Monsters: the life of James Whale*

1. A Universal publicity poster

ALL QUIET ON THE WESTERN FRONT

The Story of a Film

Andrew Kelly

I.B. Tauris *Publishers*
LONDON · NEW YORK

Published in paperback in 2002 by I.B.Tauris & Co Ltd
6 Salem Road, London W2 4BU
175 Fifth Avenue, New York NY 10010
www.ibtauris.com

In the United States of America and in Canada distributed by
St Martin's Press, 175 Fifth Avenue, New York NY 10010

First published in 1998

A full CIP record for this book is available from the British Library
A full CIP record for this book is available from the Library of
Congress

ISBN 1 86064 656 5

Library of Congress catalog card number: available

Printed and bound in Great Britain by MPG Books Ltd, Bodmin
Set in Monotype Garamond by Ewan Smith, London

Contents

For my parents

Illustrations

Acknowledgements

Many people have been of assistance with this book over the past five years. Librarians and archivists, in many institutions and in many countries, have been of great help in locating material. I would like to thank library staff in Bradford Central Library, the British Film Institute, the Margaret Herrick Library in the Academy of Motion Picture Arts and Sciences – in particular Howard Prouty, Sam Gill, Linda Harris Mehr – Ned Comstock at the University of Southern California (for particular help with Universal archive material), Nicole Schmitt in France and staff in censor offices and film archives in Australia, New Zealand, the Netherlands, Sweden, Germany, Austria, Italy and Belgium.

For help in seeing films – in particular the many versions of *All Quiet on the Western Front* – I would like to thank Jürgen Labenski, Bob Gitt, the National Film Archive, and Patrick Sheehan and David Parker in the Library of Congress. For translation of French and Scandinavian material I would like to thank David Fox and Patrick Litherland.

Philippa Brewster had confidence in this book and has supported its publication. She has also been an editor of great value and a colleague and a friend. For invaluable comments on various drafts of this book – and for additional help – I would like to thank, in no particular order, Jeffrey Richards, Barry Taylor, Melanie Kelly (who has lived with this book for a long time),

Natasha Fraser, James Pepper, James Robertson, Luke Mckernan, Bob Baker, Jim Sheehan, Rachel Phillips, Nicholas Reeves, Jerry Ohlinger and Peter van den Dungen.

James Curtis, Kevin Brownlow, and Thomas Schneider have been of particular assistance in providing information, chasing and checking facts, challenging assertions: this book is all the more stronger for their contributions.

None of these are responsible for any errors in this book. The help of all these people, over many years, should have minimised these. Needless to say, any that remain are my responsibility.

I am grateful to those holders of copyright material who have given permission for material to be included in this book. Kevin Brownlow has allowed me to quote extensively from his work, and has given me access to his interviews with Lewis Milestone, William Bakewell and Harold Goodwin. Thomas Schneider has allowed me to use interview material. Teresa Hooley's poem 'A War Film' from *Scars Upon My Heart* has been reproduced courtesy of Jonathan Cape. Permission to quote Curt Riess and Billy Wilder has been granted by Julie Gilbert from her book *Opposite Attraction: the lives of Erich Maria Remarque and Paulette Goddard* (Pantheon, 1995). Material from interviews with Michael Blake has been used with the permission of James Curtis. The poem 'The War Films' by Henry Newbolt has been reproduced courtesy of Peter Newbolt.

Extracts from the 1930 release of *All Quiet on the Western Front* are © 1930 by Universal City Studios, Inc. Extracts from the 1930 silent version of the film are © 1930 by Universal City Studios, Inc. Extracts from the 1939 version of the film are © 1939 by Universal City Studios. In all cases these quotes are courtesy of Universal Publishing Rights, a Division of Universal Licensing, Inc. All rights reserved. I am grateful to Christiane Townsend of Universal Studios for assistance with this.

Film stills appear by courtesy of the British Film Institute, the

Erich Maria Remarque Archive and the Wisconsin Center for Film and Theater Research. Thanks are due to staff in all three organisations. The picture of the advertisement for *All Quiet on the Western Front* on the Dunedin tram (p. 103) is from the Jack Welsh Collection, New Zealand Film Archive. I am grateful to Diane Pivac from the Film Archive for her assistance with this.

All attempts have been made to locate copyright holders of material used in this book. If any attribution or acknowledgement is missing it would be appreciated if contact could be made, care of the publishers, so that this can be rectified in any future edition.

When first released, the film was exactly the way I wanted it ... *All Quiet* had rough sledding in many countries and in some was forbidden exhibition. But I'm glad to report that the picture proved to have a longer life than many a politician and is still going strong in spite of brutal cutting, stupid censors and bigoted politicos.

Lewis Milestone, 1964

Introduction

I first saw *All Quiet on the Western Front* when I was eleven years old. I was staying at my brother's house, it was on television that night, and he told me that I should watch it (he was a bit of a film buff). It was very late, I recall, and well past the time I normally went to bed. But this was before the availability of video, and we were reading the book at school. So I stayed up. It proved to be a defining moment in my life: I was captivated right from the start of the film; by the end I had been moved more profoundly than I have ever been before or since.

For much of the twentieth century the movies have been the most popular of the arts – a magical form of entertainment, an education, a power for good and bad, an arm of government and an embodiment of the democratic spirit. Those of us who have been captured by the cinema never really lose the love we have for the communal experience, for the dark, for the poetry – 'the picture dancing on a screen', as Siegfried Sassoon said.[1] In *The Moviegoer* Walker Percy talks about the importance of the movies: 'The fact is I am quite happy in a movie, even a bad movie,' he says.

Other people, so I have read, treasure memorable moments in their lives: the time one climbed the Parthenon at sunrise, the summer night one met a lonely girl in Central Park and achieved with her a sweet and natural relationship, as they say in books. I too once met a girl in Central Park, but it is not much to remember. What I remember is the time John Wayne killed three men with a carbine as he was falling to the dusty street in *Stagecoach*, and the time the kitten found Orson Welles in the doorway in *The Third Man*.[2]

I remember these moments – just as I remember Rock Hudson and Jane Wyman falling in love in *All That Heaven Allows*, Paul Henreid leading the Marseillaise in *Casablanca*, Jean Simmons singing 'Let Him Go, Let Him Tarry' in *The Way to the Stars* and Ginger Rogers dancing the black bottom in *Roxie Hart*. Most of all, though, I remember the outstretched hand of Paul Bäumer at the culmination of *All Quiet on the Western Front* – a hand symbolising bright, beautiful youth decimated by that ugly, brutal and pointless war.

I did not know then that it was not Lew Ayres' hand (it was that of Lewis Milestone, the director). I was unaware that this was not the full version. Nor did I appreciate until a long time later that the version of the book we had been given to read for our English class had been edited to remove material regarded as inappropriate for young minds. But even if I had it would not have mattered: though the film was cut, and the book censored, they still provoked emotion and tears.

Having seen *All Quiet on the Western Front* I became a pacifist. Later I discovered that Lew Ayres, the star of the film, was a pacifist. Later still, I realised that, whilst war was wrong, and the First World War an abomination, a waste of a nation's youth, the pacifist option was not an appropriate stance to take in the Second World War (I hope that I would have opposed the war in 1914, and been a supporter in 1939).

But *All Quiet on the Western Front* has stayed with me and continues to influence me today. Do I share this with many people? It is said in articles and reviews that a billion people have seen the film. It is impossible to say how many people have seen it – whatever the numbers, it has had a profound influence on me, and my view of art, and of life, has often been affected by my viewing of the film. This link can be obvious: after reading Remarque's book I searched out the prose and poetry of the war (which play a large part in the discussion of the film in this book) and the battle-scarred landscapes of Paul Nash remind me of Milestone's almost unique achievement in recreating, in such a convincing way, the trenches and No Man's Land of the Western Front. But it is sometimes surprising. When I read A. E. Housman's *A Shropshire Lad* I thought of Detering, one of the older troops, who left the trenches to go home. Detering had spoken of his love for the cherry blossom and his friends speculated that he had seen it again and wanted to go back to his farm. Indeed, Housman could have written the poem for him:

Loveliest of trees, the cherry now
Is hung with bloom along the bough,
And stands about the woodland ride
Wearing white for Eastertide.

Now, of my threescore years and ten,
Twenty will not come again,
And take from seventy springs a score,
It only leaves me fifty more.

And since to look at things in bloom
Fifty springs are little room,
About the woodlands I will go
To see the cherry hung with snow.

I know that I share this memory with many people. I know from the correspondence I have had with archivists, historians, and writers that they remember the film in the same way that I do. It influenced the film director Joseph Losey so much that he wanted to use the ending to begin his own anti-war film, *King and Country* (1964 – Milestone persuaded him not to do this as it would open his film to ridicule and, in any case, Universal would not allow such use). The Payne Fund study into American children's attitudes towards cinema conducted between 1929 and 1932 – still the one piece of detailed investigation into the impact of the cinema – highlighted that some who had viewed *All Quiet on the Western Front* afterwards opposed war. Samuel Hynes, talking about the formation of views about the war in Britain, said that films such as *Journey's End* (1930), *The Dawn Patrol* (1930), *Hell's Angels* (1930) *Westfront 1918* (1930), as well as *All Quiet on the Western Front*, 'were all part of the myth-making process in Britain, and one must suppose that more British men and women formed their ideas of the Great War from these films than from all the war books put together.'[3]

And their participation in the film proved to be a great moment in the lives of those who took part, as William Bakewell, one of the actors, recalled in 1991:

> More than sixty years have passed since we crawled around in the mud. … *All Quiet on the Western Front* remains a vivid milestone … in the professional lives of all of us who shared the experience. No matter what other pictures or sets we have worked on during all those years, there was invariably someone who would come up to us and say: 'Remember when we were on *All Quiet*?' Maybe it would be an actor, maybe an electrician, maybe a grip. We had become a kind of fraternity … It has remained in the forefront of the great film classics. And we wouldn't have missed it for anything.[4]

All Quiet on the Western Front was not the first war film, nor the first anti-war film, but it is the greatest of all war films, 'the most powerful indictment of war's stupidity, waste, carnage, agony and confusion yet captured on film', as one 1960s commentator said.[5] Hollywood, to the surprise of many, had made a great film, recognised by the Academy Award for best picture in 1930. But there is a darker side: like the book that preceded it, *All Quiet on the Western Front* was hugely controversial, in particular in the author's native Germany, where it became the source of political conflict.

Many myths surround *All Quiet on the Western Front*, book, author and film, which are difficult to correct after so many years. Part of the problem is that publishers and film studios, in hyping their publications and films, often resort to fanciful accounts; correspondingly, there has been little interest until recently in maintaining documentation and archives. Remarque complained about all the myths surrounding him: that his real name was Kramer; that he was a French Jew; that the manuscript was first offered to a conservative publisher and, after rejection, was changed into a pacifist novel; that he had never been a soldier; that he had served, but as a Frenchman!

The history of the film suffers also from such myths: it was reported, for example, in a Danish newspaper in the late 1960s that Carl Brisson, a Danish actor who worked in Britain, had been offered the lead role (this is unlikely); that it started as a silent production and then turned into a sound film; that ZaSu Pitts played the mother in the released silent version (untrue, though she is in the trailer for this); that the film was nominated in 1936 for the Nobel Peace Prize (which it wasn't and couldn't have been, as films are not eligible).

This book has tried to tell the full story of *All Quiet on the Western Front*. It has involved research in film libraries, censorship offices and studio archives around the world, and investigation of the memoirs of those involved; the author has interviewed one of the actors (who is now dead – there are no other surviving actors from the film) and used other interviews where available; the book uses newspaper articles and reviews from many countries. It is a full story. It would be foolhardy to say, however, that what has resulted is the final word – this is simply not possible in any endeavour to write history, and most of all in a business where much has been built on myth.

Chapter 1 sets *All Quiet on the Western Front* in context, with an analysis of cinema and the First World War, focusing particularly on propaganda and the turn against conflict in the late 1920s and early 1930s (the position that remains today). Chapter 2 covers the history of the book upon which the film was based and its author, Erich Maria Remarque. The two chapters that follow look in detail at the production of the film: the first reports on those who were involved – the 'boys of *All Quiet*' as one of the stars described them; the second on the difficulties involved in the preparation of the screenplay and the logistical problems of making a film about war in the early sound period. Chapter 5 looks at the reception for *All Quiet on the Western Front*, the controversy over its release, and the censorship and bans in many countries. Chapter 6 develops this further with the history of the film after 1930, and the story of the two other films of Remarque's trilogy about the war, *The Road Back* (1937) and *Three Comrades* (1938). The final chapter examines the greatness of *All Quiet on the Western Front* and situates it within the anti-war poetry and prose of the Great War.

This is, in many ways, a sad story. What started as a triumphant attempt to bring the true horror of warfare to the Hollywood screen turned into worldwide controversy, widespread censorship and political bans. What is this film which has moved millions and influenced and frightened governments? We turn, first, to the triumphant première in Hollywood and then to a very different reception in Germany later that year.

April 21, 1930, Carthay Circle Theatre, Los Angeles: an excited audience attends the première of *All Quiet on the Western Front*. Anticipation is high – all the signs are that this is a major event. As they enter the packed cinema, they are greeted by a corps of US Marines. William De Mille, President of the Academy of Motion Picture Arts and Sciences, addresses the audience as head of ceremonies and introduces the stars of the film. All the main actors and technical staff are present, although, curiously, Lewis Milestone, the director, is absent, travelling on a train east and then on to Europe – he was nervous and concerned that the audience, horrified at the portrayal of the war, would walk out. Following a newsreel, a cartoon based on one of *Aesop's Fables* and a performance by Abe Lyman and his band, the lights go down, the curtains open, and, after the credits, the following words appear over music:

> This story is neither an accusation nor a confession, and least of all an adventure, for death is not an adventure to those who stand face to face with it. It will try simply to tell of a generation of men who, even though they may have escaped its shells, were destroyed by the war.[6]

It is the early days of the war and troops are being mobilised amidst scenes of great jubilation in a small German town. Himmelstoss (John Wray) the mild-mannered village postman and Meyer (Edmund Breese) the butcher both agree it will all be over within a few months. At school, Kantorek (Arnold Lucy) the patriotic teacher speaks of the romance and glory of the war and the need to defend the Fatherland:

> Now, my beloved class, this is what we must do. Strike with all our power, use every ounce of strength to win victory before the end of the year. ... You are the life of the Fatherland. ... You are the iron men of Germany. You are the gay heroes who will repulse the enemy. ... It is not for me to suggest that any of you should stand up and offer to defend his country. But I wonder if such a thing is going through your heads? I know that in one of the schools the boys have risen up in the classroom and enlisted in a mass, and of course, if such a thing should happen here, you would not blame me for a feeling of pride.

And shortly after:

> I believe it will be a quick war, that there will be few losses, but if losses there must be, then let us remember the Latin phrase which must have come to the lips of many a Roman when he stood embattled in a foreign land, 'Dulce et

2. Troops mobilising for war in *All Quiet on the Western Front*
(author's collection)

decorum est pro patria mori'. Sweet and fitting it is to die
for the Fatherland.

Most of the boys are impressed. Kemmerich (Ben Alexander)
imagines the glory of wearing uniform and Leer (Scott Kolk)

daydreams about the women who will be attracted to him when he is a soldier. Only Behm (Walter Browne Rogers) is worried and has to be persuaded by the others. Following their leader, Paul Bäumer (Lew Ayres), the whole class enlists, although the glory is soon shattered when they reach training camp. They meet up again with Himmelstoss, now a sadistic drill sergeant, who forces them to crawl many times through mud and humiliates them throughout. They obtain revenge that night by beating him as he stumbles back to barracks drunk. The soldiers move up, receiving their first taste of war when the railway station is bombed.

Arriving at their billets they meet some already hardened and cynical veterans of the war: Katczinsky – Kat (Louis Wolheim), Tjaden (George 'Slim' Summerville), Detering (Harold Goodwin) and Westhus (Richard Alexander). Wiring duty follows and, as shells fall nearby, the young recruits are scared. Behm fouls himself. Bäumer nervously places his arm round Kat's shoulders as Kat tells them all how to survive against the shells. As wiring commences, however, there is a bombardment. Behm, frightened, runs out of the trench and is killed.

The troops then move to the trenches, where their nerves are shattered by a bombardment lasting for five days. The French attack and, in a series of brutal battles, half the company are either killed or injured for no gain in territory. At one point Bäumer sees two severed hands gripping barbed wire after an explosion has torn an advancing soldier apart.

A welcome break follows, although the cook refuses at first to serve the meal as only half the company are present. He is forced by a senior officer to serve the food, and the soldiers retreat to a riverbank where they discuss the causes of war as they eat. After eating they visit the injured Kemmerich and discover that his leg has been amputated. Paul is trying to comfort him as he dies. A number of other classmates are then killed, Kemmerich's boots passing to each in turn.

A second major battle follows. As the troops wait in the dugout, Himmelstoss arrives in the trench. He bullies a young soldier, but his attempts to take command are greeted with derision. The assault then begins: Himmelstoss goes over the top but stumbles into a shell-hole where Paul accuses him of cowardice. Ordered to advance by a senior officer, they run forward and Himmelstoss dies. Paul is caught in a shell-hole where he fatally stabs Duval, a French soldier (Raymond Griffith), but is forced to stay with him for two days. When the Frenchman dies, Paul promises to help his family after the war:

> when you jumped in here, you were my enemy. And I was afraid of you. But you're just a man like me. And I killed you. Forgive me, comrade. Say that for me. Say you forgive me. No, no. You're dead. You're better off than I am. You're through. They can't do any more to you now. Oh, God! Why did they do this to us? We only wanted to live – you and I – why should they send us out to fight each other? If we threw away these rifles and these uniforms you could be my brother just like Kat and Albert. You have to forgive me, comrade. I'll do all I can. I'll write to your parents. ... I'll write to your wife. ... I promise she'll not want for anything. And I'll help her and your parents too. Only forgive me. Forgive me.

Paul manages, eventually, to crawl to safety, where he is comforted by Kat.

Later they march into a new town. Whilst bathing in a river, Paul, Albert (William Bakewell), and Leer see three French women who tell them to visit that night. Tjaden is also invited but the others persuade Kat to get him drunk. The three spend the night with the women. The following morning they march out of the town, but are attacked, and both Paul and Albert are injured. In the hospital, Albert's leg is amputated, but Paul, to everyone's surprise (he has been taken to the dying room), recovers and is allowed home leave.

Back home the cheering crowds have gone and the streets are deserted except for some injured veterans. Paul finds his mother (Beryl Mercer) ill, and there is little food. He goes to meet his

father in a beer-garden. There he is told how to win the war, but
he leaves as his father and his friends argue amongst themselves.
As he walks up the street he hears Kantorek once again attempting to get the class to enlist:

> From the farms they have gone. From the schools, from the
> factories. They have gone, bravely, nobly, ever forward
> realising that there is no other duty now but to save the
> Fatherland. The age of enlistment is now 16 years, and
> though you are barely men, your country needs you for the
> greatest service a citizen can give.

Paul has arrived at an opportune time for Kantorek:

> as if to prove all I have said, here is one of the first to go
> … a lad who sat before me on these very benches, who gave
> up all to serve in the first year of the war; one of the Iron
> Youth who have made Germany invincible in the field. Look
> at him, sturdy and bronzed and clear-eyed. The kind of
> soldier every one of you should envy.

He asks Paul to speak to the impressed class. Paul is reluctant
at first but, when pressed, admits there is little he can say that
the class does not already know: 'We live in the trenches out
there. We fight and try not to be killed; but sometimes we are.
That's all.' This is not what Kantorek wishes to hear and Paul
begins to get angry. He remembers the teacher's original speech
to the class and knows after his experiences that 'Pro patria mori'
– the old lie, as Wilfred Owen characterised it – is horribly wrong:

> I heard you in here reciting that same old stuff. Making more
> iron men. More young heroes. You still think it's beautiful
> and sweet to die for your country. … Well, we used to think
> you knew; but the first bombardment taught us better! It's
> dirty and painful to die for your country. When it comes to
> dying for your country, it's better not to die at all.

Accused of cowardice by members of the class, Bäumer turns

on them: 'Three years we've had of it … four years! And every day a year and every night a century. And our bodies are earth and our thoughts are clay, and we sleep and eat with death.'

He is accused of cowardice, and he returns to the front even though his leave is yet to finish. Meeting up with the company he finds that only Tjaden and Kat are alive. He meets Kat as he searches for food but Kat is injured and dies as Paul carries him back. Paul dies in the last few weeks of the war, shot by a sniper as he tries to reach for a butterfly. The ghostly figures of the dead soldiers march towards the sky over hundreds of crosses and graves.

No applause greeted the end of the film – the audience seemed shocked and disturbed, 'groggy with an excess of emotion', as Louella Parsons, reviewer (and later gossip columnist), wrote in the *Los Angeles Examiner.*[7] John Barrymore, the great actor, turned to George Cukor and said, 'You see – great pictures can be made in this town.'[8] Some of the audience then departed for an invitation-only party hosted by Carl Laemmle Junior, the film's producer.

The position is very different seven months later. Again a packed, eager audience awaits the première of *All Quiet on the Western Front*, only this time it is in Germany, at the Mozart Hall in Berlin. There are high expectations: the film has already won two Academy Awards and has been praised wherever it has been released. But it is also controversial – based on the best-selling novel by a German, a book that has provoked a widespread debate in the country, the film has not been received well by German critics following the preview the night before. It is also a time of political turmoil, with recent electoral success by the Nazis only heightening the fever. It is little wonder that one commentator said that 'the audience came that evening to Mozart Hall not just to see a movie but to participate in a major cultural and political event.'[9]

Trouble started after one reel, when Joseph Goebbels left the auditorium signalling to his Brown Shirt cronies to start the riot. The Nazi had been looking forward to this. Two days earlier in his diary he had noted, 'On Friday we're going to see *All Quiet on the Western Front*. This should teach the eunuchs some manners. I'm very happy about it.'[10] Shouting 'Judenfilm', the protesters released mice, stink-bombs and sneezing powder in the auditorium. Order was soon restored and the cinema was cleared.

Goebbels continued to foment protest for another four nights to keep the film from being shown. The Nazis – and, it should be said, some patriots – objected to the film because of what they saw as an attack on Germany. But it was also an illustration of how powerful cinema was regarded as being and of how intertwined it had become with the First World War, international politics and propaganda. Chapter 1 examines this relationship, the Myth of the War and the way cinema went from being an arm of national government to become the prime mechanism for transmitting anti-war views to millions of people around the world.

1

Cinema, Society and the First World War

With eight-and-a-half million dead, and twenty million injured, the First World War was a disaster unparalleled in human history. There was nothing great about the Great War except the scale of despair and destruction. Nor was there victory. Those who had celebrated the defeat of Germany soon learned that they, too, had suffered – bitter memories, dead and injured relatives and friends, promises betrayed. In her book on the first months of the war, *The Guns of August*, Barbara Tuchman concluded that 'the war had many diverse results and one dominant one transcending all others: disillusion'.[1]

Disillusion is part of what Samuel Hynes calls the Myth of the War – 'not a falsification of reality, but an imaginative version of it, the story of the war that has evolved, and has come to be expected as true':

> a generation of innocent young men, their heads full of high abstractions like Honour, Glory, and England, went off to war to make the world safe for democracy. They were slaughtered in stupid battles planned by stupid generals. Those who survived were shocked, disillusioned and embittered by their war experiences, and saw that their real

3. The front line of war in *All Quiet on the Western Front*
(author's collection)

enemies were not the Germans, but the old men at home
who had lied to them. They rejected the values of the society
that had sent them to war, and in doing so separated their
own generation from the past and from their cultural in-
heritance.[2]

Contributions to the development of the Myth ranged widely,
but a key part was culture: the *art* of the war – poetry and prose
(in the work of Wilfred Owen, Siegfried Sassoon and the anti-
war novelists of the 1920s), paintings (Paul Nash), photographs
and films. And it is this art which has dominated perceptions of
the war since 1918 and which continues to mould the conscience
and the imagination today. Although it is eighty years since the
end of the war, the popular and critical success of such recent
novels as Sebastian Faulks' *Birdsong* and Pat Barker's *Regeneration*
trilogy in Britain, and Sebastien Japrisot's French story of five

soldiers thrown into No Man's Land to die, *A Very Long Engagement* (all of which are being filmed), highlights this continuing fascination and obsession.[3]

It was the poetry of the war that was first to articulate the Myth, then the war novels and prose, and later the cinema, which also transmitted it to the greatest number. And yet it was only a few films that did this – great films, it should be said, but still only a few. And of these, *All Quiet on the Western Front* was the greatest of them all.

It was not always the case that cinema put forward an anti-war position. The film industry follows trends rather than creates them, and it is the *reflection* of the rejection of conflict that is important. Few anti-war films were made prior to 1925, and it was the force of literature in the late 1920s that propelled cinema into action. But the cinema had, by this time, already been intimately involved with the war; indeed, it had been one of the key forces for marketing the war. Between 1914 and 1918, officially and unofficially, most combatant countries brought cinema into the framework of government as a partner to sell the war at home and abroad, to maintain motivation and morale, and hence to continue to justify involvement. And it is the role of cinema in society, its ability to reach a mass audience, and its already strong history of participation which frightened censors' offices and governments around the world, and which had led the Nazis to call down such opprobrium on *All Quiet on the Western Front*.[4]

Ironically, the first film to be influential during the war was a pacifist one, although it was about an imaginary war, it was not released in Europe, and it was Danish. *Lay Down Your Arms* was based on the best-selling novel by Bertha von Suttner (a leader of the international peace movement before 1914) and written by Carl Dreyer, who was later to make some of the classic films of world cinema with *La Passion de Jeanne d'Arc* (1928) and *Day of Wrath* (1943). It should have had its première at the Twenty-First

4. Christ returns to earth to try to bring peace to the battlefields
in *Civilization* (1916) (BFI Stills, Posters and Designs)

International Peace Congress in September 1914 (a gathering of
the worldwide peace movement), but the outbreak of war had
caused its indefinite cancellation. It was, however, released in the
United States, where it became embroiled in the debate about
intervention and was used by pacifists to promote neutrality.

Although *Lay Down Your Arms* was a Danish film it did repres-
ent the first, neutral, phase in American cinema. Hollywood went
through five chronological phases: first came those films ad-
vocating, or said to advocate, neutrality (*One of Millions, Prince of
Peace* and *A Victim of War* from 1914); second, those supporting
preparedness, the most notorious, and hence important, of which
was *The Battle Cry of Peace* in 1915; third – following the entry
into war – those that favoured intervention, in which every genre
was utilised to back the war effort (family drama, romance,
espionage, adventure); fourth, in the mid-to-late 1920s, those

portraying the war as an adventure, such as the aviation classics *Wings* (1927) and *Lilac Time* (1928). Finally, there was the bitter period of the rejection of conflict typified by *All Quiet on the Western Front*. The actual release of films was not as crude as this. Whilst it is correct that a number of influential pacifist shorts and features were released up to the end of 1916, there were other films in circulation that dissented from the prevailing position. Nevertheless, many of the films made at this time did oppose intervention in Europe.

Early production was heavily influenced by President Woodrow Wilson, who was determined to keep America out of the war. Many films reflected this view, but it was Thomas Ince's *Civilization* and D. W. Griffith's *Intolerance*, both released in 1916, that were important: both were influential in American political debate and in promoting peace; both were Wilsonian in the views put forward. But they were meretricious as anti-war films. Ince's concern was always the box office (pacifism was a popular and lucrative stance in early 1916), and he was not averse to changing his film from being, supposedly, anti-war to pro-war when it was released in Britain as *Civilization, What Every True Briton Is Fighting For* in 1917.

Griffith was more honest, and *Intolerance* was a masterwork, a valiant, eloquent, unique attempt to promote peace and harmony. But his stance towards the war was ambivalent. At the London première of his film (which took place the day after America declared war on Germany) he said he was happy to know that his country would soon be fighting alongside the English, and he made the propaganda film *Hearts of the World* in 1917 for the British government. It was only after the war that his stance became consistent, and *Isn't Life Wonderful?* (1924), his eloquent study of post-war suffering in Germany, was his apology for his pro-war activities, according to the actress (and Griffith regular) Lillian Gish.

Although anti-war films followed these, the most important of which was the successful *War Brides* (1916), by now the preparedness stage was strong and the film industry was mobilised subsequently to support the expeditionary force: anti-war pictures were banned by government, movie stars sold liberty bonds, official propaganda films toured the country and any pro-German sentiment was dealt with rapidly. (Robert Goldstein was imprisoned for ten years for making what was judged to be an anti-English and hence pro-German, film in his portrayal of the American revolution, *The Spirit of '76*, in 1917. His sentence was later commuted to three years and he was released in 1920.) The mood went from 'I Didn't Raise my Boy to Be a Soldier', a hit song of the early months of the war, to *I'm Glad My Son Grew Up to Be a Soldier*, a film in late 1915. America entered the war sixteen months later.

Historians and film-makers have not looked with much sympathy on Hollywood films of the war period. Commenting on the aesthetics of the war films, Terry Ramsaye, one of the first, and still most reliable, of the film historians, said in 1926: 'The peculiar fact for screen history is that the vast experience of the war contributed nothing whatever to the art of the motion picture.'[5] For Jack Warner, writing over four decades later, even the pro-war films failed as propaganda: 'The motion picture industry was anxious to help,' he said, 'but because the government controlled the entire war film production program, there were no great inspirational pictures made.'[6]

Conversely, Louella Parsons (who was later to praise *All Quiet on the Western Front*) argued in *Photoplay* in September 1918 that the films were important in promoting opposition to German militarism:

> If German vandalism could reach overseas, the Kaiser would order every moving picture studio crushed to dust and every theatre blown to atoms. There has been no more effective ammunition aimed at the Prussian empire than ... pictures of German atrocities. ... The followers of the cinema have seen with their own eyes how German militarism is waged

against civilisation. They have seen the rape of Belgium, the devastation of France and the evil designs against America. … And while these films have been raising the temperature of the Allies' patriotism to a blood heat, Germany has been gnashing its teeth.[7]

They were also important for the future of world cinema. The American film industry had come of age by 1918: the war years witnessed the demise of European film-making and the growth of the American cinema as an artistic and entertainment force worldwide. Anita Loos – an American screenwriter (she had written the intertitles for *Intolerance*) – said that 'World War One was the reason for Hollywood'. She added: 'At the time war broke out, movies had gained a very substantial place in Europe. They were being made in France, and in Italy they were particularly good, and there was no need for Hollywood. But the war broke out and that changed the whole scene. It was impossible to work with the economics of war surrounding these studios. So I really credit Hollywood on World War One.'[8]

In common with trends worldwide, there was little coverage of the war after 1918; audiences had become tired of the subject and there was no market for war films. A turning point was 1925 with the release of *The Big Parade*, King Vidor's film of the American doughboy. Though this was not as fundamental an attack on conflict as the later anti-war classics, its considerable success, due principally to the quality of the production and to John Gilbert, the lead character, showed that war films could make money (it was the highest-grossing silent film).

Vidor's success led the way: *The Big Parade* was followed by a new generation of war films, including the classic aviation dramas, *Wings* (1927), *Hell's Angels* and *The Dawn Patrol* (both 1930) which stressed the heroism and derring-do of the war without avoiding some of the more brutal consequences of conflict. At the same time there was a more gentle coverage, with pacifism as a key theme, in such films as *Barbed Wire* (1927), *Four Sons* and *The*

Enemy (both 1928), which looked at love between enemies and the suffering at home.

There was little opportunity for an anti-war cinema to develop in Europe, as most countries were involved from the start. In England, France and Germany cinema rapidly became embroiled in propaganda.

Unlike many other European countries, in Germany film production and exhibition prospered during the war. The military blockade of the country meant that no films could be imported from the allied forces and the United States. However, there was strong demand for cinema in other parts of Europe, which created an export market for German producers. The relative health of the cinema led to the country becoming one of the leading film producers in Europe, but the propaganda value was wasted: widely reported German atrocities, such as the rape of Belgian nuns, whether real or imagined, meant that the moral initiative had been lost.

To promote more effective propaganda, the German government adopted a strongly interventionist policy towards the industry and invested directly in production companies. In 1916 it joined with a number of film companies to form Deulig – Deutsche Lichtspiel-Gesellschaft – which promoted Germany through propaganda films at home and in neutral countries. This was followed in early 1917 by the establishment of the government's own photographic and film office – Bufa, Bild- und Filmamt – which built cinemas on the Eastern and Western fronts. Another attempt to conscript the German film industry for propaganda was made with the formation of Ufa (Universum Film A. G.) in November 1917, which was financed jointly by private industry and government.

By this stage, the military had accepted the importance of film propaganda. In July 1917, General Ludendorff, the chief of staff, had written: 'The war has shown the overwhelming force of pictures and films as a medium for educating and influencing the masses. Unfortunately our enemies have used the advantage they have over us in this field so completely that we have suffered considerable damage. ... For this reason it is desirable, if the war is to be brought to a successful conclusion, to ensure that film is used to make the deepest possible impression wherever German influence is still possible.'[9]

Though Ufa's immediate objectives failed with the declaration of the Armistice, the company became established quickly as a major force domestically and in international film exhibition, where its purchase of theatres enabled the post-war boycott of German films to be broken. By this stage government investment, which had attracted considerable controversy, had been rescinded. Ufa later came under the control of the right-wing Alfred Hugenberg, who was involved in the campaign against *All Quiet on the Western Front*.

Despite such propaganda, opposition to the war had been present in German popular culture. Though there had been little agitation against the war from the peace movement (which was weak), there were poems and paintings opposing the conflict up to, and after, 1918, in particular the work of Käthe Kollwitz, John Heartfield, Otto Dix and George Grosz. However, the political turmoil of the early Weimar period seemed to occupy most people's minds. There was also the fact that, after years of poverty and misery, people simply wanted to have fun.

Anti-militarism remained an important issue, though it took some time before such sentiments influenced cinema production and exhibition (Germany was no different from other countries). In 1919, the remarkable horror film *Das Cabinet des Dr Caligari* (*The Cabinet of Dr Caligari*), the story of a mad director of a lunatic asylum and his (innocent) somnambulist Cesare, was released. This could have been one of the first post-war, anti-militarist films – its authors, Carl Mayer and Hans Janowitz (both veterans), had written the screenplay as a condemnation of war. For them, Caligari's power and disregard for human life represented military authority, and Cesare was the ordinary soldier, forced to kill, however unwittingly. However, Robert Wiene, the director, changed the story to the horror tale known so well today. Siegfried Kracauer, in his *From Caligari to Hitler*, said that this action 'perverted, if not reversed ... [the writers'] intrinsic intentions. ... [T]he original story exposed the madness inherent in authority, Wiene's *Caligari* glorified authority and convicted its antagonist of madness. A revolutionary film was thus turned into a conformist one.'[10]

A clearly identifiable anti-war film appeared two years later. *Namenlose Helden – War*, or *Nameless Heroes* – was released in the week before Armistice Day in November 1924, despite criticism from the German government, who feared that it would open the military to ridicule. The film tells the story of a working-class family driven to poverty and disaster after Scholz, the father, is conscripted. Forced to give up their home, his wife lodges with their two children in an attic, where one is killed in a fire. This disturbs Scholz so much that he is careless and is blinded in a mine explosion. His wife is also dead now, and, on returning home, he tramps the streets with his son. Scholz is shot dead when he enters a restricted area.

By the mid-to-late 1920s, Germany had recovered some of its stability and status at home and abroad. Much of the momentum for this came from a wish to overturn the humiliating Versailles settlement. A peace movement had also begun to emerge. In 1922, a rally in Berlin had attracted over ten thousand people, who proclaimed 'Never Again War'. Two years later *War against War!*, Ernst Friedrich's immensely successful book consisting mainly of horrific photographs from the conflict, was published.[11] Despite opposition from the Right, the Locarno Treaty – the non-aggression pact between Germany, Belgium and France – was successfully concluded in 1925, finalising the issue of frontiers. In 1926 Germany became a member of the League of Nations and, two years later, it signed the Kellogg–Briand Pact (in which fifteen nations renounced war). The country was once again part of the international community.

The war was not altogether absent from screens during this period, with some of the leading war films exhibited in Germany: the war adventure *What Price Glory?*, for example, enjoyed a lengthy and popular run in 1927. Domestic production, though, was limited, and any films released were predictably neutral. There was at least one covering the story of Mata Hari (in 1927), and there were two unsuccessful naval films, *Kreuzer Emden* (1926) and *U-9 Weddigen* (1927). It was to be another two years, however, before Germany made its own contribution to anti-war cinema.

In Britain, as in Germany, the cinema was a vital source of entertainment during the First World War and a crucial component of official propaganda. In the 1930s it turned against the war, though not to the same extent as other countries. The conservatism of the film establishment, censorship and the class bias of British war memoirs and films meant that the trench life portrayed in literature and on the screen offered only a limited impression of the reality of the conflict. British cinema was more Rupert Brooke than Siegfried Sassoon: the war was bloody slaughter, but the deaths that resulted were not necessarily wasted. The most eloquent views of this were the classic stage play and film, *Journey's End* (1930), and the story of Gallipoli, *Tell England* (1931).

During the war, British domestic production – in common with that of most other European countries – was heavily affected by Hollywood's expansionism, and the war had a profound impact on the industry: resources were limited, technicians and actors conscripted and income lowered by an entertainments tax and the export ban. But there were other reasons for poor production. The British industry was technologically backward and production was often affected by the climate. Above all, American films had better stars and more adventurous stories.

The government had realised from the start the need for a persuasion strategy and had appointed Charles Masterman, Chancellor of the Duchy of Lancaster, to lead the campaign. However, the first official film was not released until the end of 1915, as

Masterman had decided that propaganda would be based on fact, not fiction, and the first cinematographers did not set off for the front until October 1915. He was also hampered by the lack of support from the Admiralty and the War Office, which felt that film was a trivial, vulgar form of working-class entertainment and feared that sensitive information would be disclosed.

The most popular films were those that covered a single military operation, the best known being the 1916 release *The Battle of the Somme*. This presented an almost sympathetic view of German soldiers in a generally dispassionate production. The ultra-patriotic Sir Henry Newbolt – his 'The Vigil' (originally written in December 1897) was the first official war poem – liked the war films:

O living pictures of the dead,
    O songs without a sound,
O fellowship whose phantom tread
    Hallows a phantom ground –
How in a gleam have these revealed
    The faith we had not found.

We have sought God in a cloudy Heaven,
    We have passed by God on earth:
His seven sins and his sorrows seven,
    His wayworn mood and mirth,
Like a ragged cloak have hid from us
    The secret of his birth.

Brother of men, when now I see
    The lads go forth in line,
Thou knowest my heart is hungry in me
    As for thy bread and wine:
Thou knowest my heart is bowed in me
    To take their death for mine.

Wilfred Owen, a far better poet, called the films 'illusory'. Another poet, Teresa Hooley, described how such war films made her fear for her son (this was not published until 1927):

I saw,
With a catch of the breath and the heart's uplifting,
Sorrow and pride,
     The 'week's great draw' –
The Mons Retreat;
The 'Old Contemptibles' who fought, and died,
The horror and the anguish and the glory.

As in a dream,
Still hearing machine-guns rattle and shells scream,
I came out into the street.

When the day was done,
My little son
Wondered at bath-time why I kissed him so,
Naked upon my knee.
How could he know
The sudden terror that assaulted me? ...
The body I had borne
Nine moons beneath my heart,
A part of me ...
If, someday,
It should be taken away
To War. Tortured. Torn.
Slain.
Rotting in No Man's Land, out in the rain –
My little son ...
Yet all those men had mothers, every one.

How should he know
Why I kissed and kissed and kissed him, crooning his name?
He thought that I was daft.
He thought it was a game,
And laughed, and laughed.

The Battle of the Somme was a great success, and attracted great
praise (although, ironically, the scene that seemed to attract most

interest – that showing a soldier emerging from a trench, only to be shot and fall back – was faked[12]). The king, following a private viewing, said 'the public should see these pictures that they may have some idea of what the Army is doing, and what war means.'[13] However, not every cinema wished to cash in on the war. One Hammersmith exhibitor put in a notice outside his theatre: WE ARE NOT SHOWING THE BATTLE OF THE SOMME. THIS IS A PLACE OF AMUSEMENT, NOT A CHAMBER OF HORRORS.[14]

The use of film in Britain became more widespread after 1917, when domestic morale was low. Propaganda units were reorganised and use began to be made of the fiction film. In addition to D. W. Griffith's *Hearts of the World*, Herbert Brenon – director of the pacifist *War Brides* – was invited to make *The National Film*, known also as *The Invasion of Britain*, a feature speculating on life in an England under German occupation. This was a troubled film: the only print was lost in a fire in June 1918 and the remake was not completed until just before the Armistice. Then distribution was postponed because of its anti-German bias, and sixteen months later it was destroyed on Treasury instructions.

Between 1918 and 1925 cinema's coverage of the war mirrored that of most other countries. Generally the subject was disliked, though this was as much to do with recession in the industry as realisation that the public wished to avoid the subject. The few productions that did result were generally lacklustre work from an unconfident and underfinanced industry. Given this background, it is surprising that any films about the war were made at all. Bucking the trend were the popular war reconstructions produced by Harry Bruce Woolfe's company British Instructional Films: *The Battle of Jutland* (1921), *Armageddon*, *Zeebrugge* (both 1924), *Ypres* (1925), *Mons* (1926) and, in 1927, the most important of them all, *The Battles of the Coronel and Falkland Islands*. Two similar films – *The Somme* and *'Q' Ships* – were released by New Era in 1927 and 1928.

To produce such films needed government approval, which was given. However, they were opposed by some members of the

Labour opposition, who said that such assistance was 'derogatory to His Majesty's uniform and ... open to grave objection as mischievous propaganda'.[15] One of the most intelligent film critics of the time, Bryher, an English novelist resident in Switzerland, criticised *The Battles of the Coronel and the Falkland Islands* in the avant-garde journal *Close Up* (which she edited):

> We want a race that understands what acceptance of warfare means. By all means let us have war films. Only let us have war straight and as it is; mainly disease and discomfort, almost always destructive (even in after civil life) in its effects. Let us get away from this nursery formula that to be in uniform is to be a hero; that brutality and waste are not to be condemned provided they are disguised in flags, medals and cheering.[16]

British fictional films about the war appeared after 1918, though they were few in number. Initially, it was hard to discard the prejudice built up over four years of bitter conflict. During the immediate post-war period, foreign features were shown, although German product was excluded under a ten-year import ban imposed in 1918 (this was lifted in 1920, but it was to be another three years before the first films arrived). Both *J'accuse* (1919 – see later) and *The Four Horsemen of the Apocalypse* (1921), the film that made Rudolph Valentino a star, were well received and avoided censorship, though *J'accuse* was not shown outside London. In April 1925 *Hearts of the World* was re-released whilst negotiations for the Locarno Treaty were at a crucial stage. German protests led the Foreign Office, in an uncharacteristic move, to intervene, and two of the more controversial sections were deleted.

There was dissent also the following year with Vidor's *The Big Parade* and another American production, *The Unknown Soldier*, Renaud Hoffman's film about a shell-shocked amnesiac soldier. Vidor's film was eventually released (exhibitors defied nationalistic protest from the British press), but objections from patriotic organisations to Hollywood hijacking British traditions – the title and film showing the burial of an unknown soldier at Arlington Cemetery – threatened to delay the latter. Despite petitions to the Home Secretary and the British Board of Film Censors (BBFC), the body responsible for awarding certificates to allow films to be shown, the film was exhibited. Other American productions did suffer at the censor's hands: both *What Price Glory?* and *Wings* had material deleted and *Hell's Angels* lost almost thirty-five minutes. The only British war film to be banned before 1925 was the 1922 production, *The Betrayal of Lord Kitchener*. The BBFC had stopped exhibition of the film because it was regarded as inaccurate. It was also banned in France and the United States following intervention from the Foreign Office.

With one exception, all other British films in the twelve years after the Armistice proved to be less controversial than those from Hollywood. These included *Mademoiselle from Armentières* (1926); *Roses of Picardy*, a 1927 production of two novels by R. H. Mottram about the love between an English officer and a French farmer's daughter in Flanders; and an expensive production of Maurice Maeterlinck's story *The Burgomaster of Stilemonde* (1929), which told of German atrocities against hostages in their custody. More ambitious and critically praised was Madeleine Carroll's first film, *The Guns of Loos*, directed by Sinclair Hill and released in 1928, about a blind veteran who returns to manage an industrial empire. One of the most interesting, and financially successful, war films of the late 1920s was Adrian Brunel's *Blighty*, the story of an officer who, after the Armistice, returns to his old job as a chauffeur. Brunel described it as 'quietly, an anti-war picture'.[17]

By far the most important British film about the war before 1930, and one of the censorship controversies of the period, was Herbert Wilcox's 1928 release, *Dawn*, the story of the life and execution of Edith Cavell, which was banned by the BBFC on the grounds that it would damage Anglo-German relations (it was banned subsequently in Holland, Australia and Ontario as undesirable and inaccurate). Ironically, Wilcox, a war veteran, had attempted throughout to avoid anti-German stereotypes: all German characters are treated sympathetically and some are portrayed as humanitarian. Wilcox remade the story in 1939 for RKO as *Nurse Edith Cavell* and was criticised again; he had wanted to make an anti-war film but was accused by many of making propaganda for the Second World War.

In common with many countries, in the late 1920s and early 1930s there was a turn against war in Britain. Building on the 1927 Kellogg–Briand Pact and the 1932 disarmament conference, considerable anti-war and pacifist sentiment developed. The League of Nations and the concept of collective security were never more popular. It was a time which saw the publication of Vera Brittain's *Testament of Youth* (she had been devastated by the loss of her brother, her fiancé and her friends in the war and had turned to pacifism and her book was a hugely influential bestseller both at the time and in the 1980s, when it was reissued and filmed as a television drama); when the Oxford Union could agree in 1933 in an influential vote that it would fight for neither king nor country; and when the Peace Pledge Union, within two years of formation, could sign up over one hundred thousand members who agreed to 'renounce war and never again ... support or sanction another'.

Cinema in France went through a phase similar to those of Germany and Britain. The domestic industry, a leader in world cinema prior to 1914, collapsed virtually overnight as technicians and actors departed for the front, film companies produced propaganda (which audiences tired of quickly) and Hollywood product swept the country. However, there is a major difference: near the end of the war, Abel Gance, with the assistance of the French army, began production of his anti-war film *J'accuse*.

That it was France where the first anti-war film should have been produced after American intervention, and *before* the Armistice, is not surprising: of all countries France had suffered the most in the war. As historian Eugen Weber states in *The Hollow Years*:

For fifty-one months ... [after August 1914] 1,000 French-
men were killed day after day, nearly 1 of every 5 mobilized,
10.5 percent of the country's active male population. That
was more than any other Western belligerent would suffer:
The British counted half as many dead and missing, Germans and Austro-Hungarians, who had incurred heavy losses,
never got as far as 10 percent. About 1,400,000 French lost
their lives; well over 1,000,000 had been gassed, disfigured,
mangled, amputated, left permanent invalids. Wheelchairs,
crutches, empty sleeves dangling loosely or tucked into
pockets became common sights. More than that had suffered
some sort of wound: Half of the 6,500,000 who survived
the war had sustained injuries. Most visible, 1,100,000, were
those who had been evidently diminished and were described
as *mutilés*, a term the dictionary translates as 'maimed' or
'mangled', and English usage prefers to clothe it in an
euphemism: 'disabled'.[18]

Gance had been influenced by his front-line experience as a
cinematographer, the deaths of many of his friends in combat,
and by Henri Barbusse's anti-war novel *Le Feu* (*Under Fire*). He
told Kevin Brownlow many years later that he was against war
because it 'is foolish': 'Ten or twenty years afterward, one reflects
that millions have died and all for nothing. One has found friends
among one's old enemies, and enemies among one's friends. ...
One doesn't have the right to play with people's lives. People's
lives are sacred.'[19]

His film, one of the most moving to have been made about
the war, was about the dead. It includes a scene where those who
have been killed rise up to question and challenge those still
alive. In Gance's book of the film (published in 1922), Jean, one
of the lead characters, describes what happened:

I was on sentry duty on the battlefield. ... All your dead
were there, all your cherished dead. Then a miracle happened;
a soldier near me slowly rose to his feet under the moon. I

5. The dead of war rise up to accuse those who sent them to their
deaths in *J'accuse*, Abel Gance's plea for an end to war (1919)
(BFI Stills, Posters and Designs)

started to run, terrified, but suddenly the dead man spoke. I
heard him say, 'Comrades, we must know if we have been
of any use! Let us go and judge whether the people are
worthy of us, of our sacrifice! Rise up! Rise up, all of you!'
And the dead obeyed. I ran in front of them to forewarn
you. They're on the march! They're coming! They will be here
soon and you will have to answer for yourselves! They will
return to their resting places with joy if their sacrifice has
been to some purpose.[20]

Gance's film is creative, powerful and poignant. The poignancy
is strengthened when it is known that the French army provided
two thousand fighting soldiers for the return of the dead
sequence. They came from Verdun and had been lucky to survive.
Within a few weeks of their return to the front 80 per cent had

been killed. As Gance said, they had played the dead probably knowing that they would soon be dead themselves.

French cinema looked critically at the war in the late 1920s, with *Verdun, visions d'histoire* (1928) and *Les Croix de bois* (*Wooden Crosses*), four years later, based on the bestselling novel by Roland Dorgelès. The film was bought by Fox, and the battle footage was used in 1936 by Howard Hawks in another version of the story, *The Road to Glory*. It was not until 1937, however, that French cinema provided its own contribution to the pantheon of anti-war cinema with *La Grande Illusion*, Jean Renoir's great humanitarian examination of the causes of war.

The year 1930 proved to be an *annus mirabilis* for the anti-war film. It saw the release not just of *All Quiet on the Western Front* but also of *Journey's End* and *Westfront 1918*. These three have often been reviewed together.

Based on the stage success of its day by R. C. Sherriff, *Journey's End* was, as Michael Balcon said, 'one of the rare films that had something to say at that particular time'.[21] In March 1918 the newly commissioned Second Lieutenant James Raleigh (David Manners) arrives eagerly at the British trenches in St Quentin, where he joins the company commanded by his old schoolfriend, Captain Dennis Stanhope MC (Colin Clive). He is met by Lieutenant Osborne (Ian Maclaren) – affectionately known as Uncle – and tells him of his love for Stanhope's sister. He also meets Trotter (Billy Bevan), a jolly, crude fellow; Hibbert (Anthony Bushell), who is affected by neuralgia and contriving to get leave; and Mason (Charles Gerrard), the cook obsessed with food and pleasing his commander.

Stanhope has been affected badly by the war and he fears that Raleigh will tell his sister of his drinking. He warns him that all letters are censored, though the first he sees contains nothing but praise for him. The next day the colonel orders Stanhope to capture a German. Osborne and Raleigh lead the raid and a gunner is taken prisoner. To Stanhope's dismay, Osborne is killed,

6. Lieutenant Osborne (Ian Maclaren) with Captain Dennis Stanhope (Colin Clive), who endures the burdens of command with drink in *Journey's End* (1930) (BFI Stills, Posters and Designs)

though that night they celebrate the success of the raid with champagne. Stanhope gets very drunk, but is disgusted when Raleigh refuses to join them. They are reconciled the next day after Raleigh has been fatally wounded. As Stanhope leaves, a bomb destroys the trench.

Whilst many have followed Balcon's claim that *Journey's End* was pacifist in outlook, Sherriff was keen not to have his work portrayed in this way. He said *Journey's End* was a play 'in which not a word was spoken against the war, in which no word of condemnation was uttered by any of its characters'.[22] This is surely wrong: whilst the film may lack the militancy of *All Quiet on the Western Front*, it is impossible to watch it without believing war is hell: the waste and slaughter of the trenches, the intolerable burdens placed on the men in command at the front and the ultimate tragedy emphasise the futility of it all. There is no patriotism or pronouncement of war aims in the film, just as there was no patriotism in the trenches. There are few epithets thrown at the Germans; when adversaries are mentioned it is done sympathetically.

However, one of the problems with the suffering portrayed in both the film and the play is that it is endured almost totally by members of the upper class. Their nobility enables them to face the hell stoically. They behave decently and with honour whilst the working-class characters provide comic resignation to the conflict (and light relief for the audience). This was a result, in part, of Sherriff's beliefs; but it was also because most British memoirs of the conflict were written by the officer class.

The key point to emerge from *Journey's End* is the impact of the war on those in command at the front line. Robert Graves said that the average time spent by an infantry subaltern on the Western Front was at some stages only three months – by then, the soldier had been either killed or wounded.[23] Knowing this was enough of a burden, but for those who had served for years, or had been wounded and then returned to the front (as was the case for many), the pressure was intolerable.

Germany's prime contribution to anti-war cinema were the two films made by G. W. Pabst in 1930 and 1931: *Westfront 1918* and *Kameradschaft*. Pabst was a pacifist, an internationalist, a 'film apostle of idealistic brotherhood between nations', as one commentator has said,[24] and one of the world's leading directors.

Westfront 1918 was based on the eloquent, though grim and bitter, book *Vier von der Infanterie* by Ernst Johannsen. It was dedicated 'In Memory of the Slain' and has as its prologue the statement *Unto Death*: 'THEY marched, these Four, in sun, and rain and wind, – in mud of the roads, in ice and snow – through flowering lands, through the desolate waste – by day, by night, to victories and terrible loss.' And it ends with: 'They fought, and knew not to what end; they died without hope, without consola-

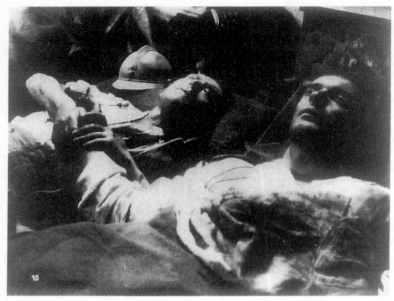

7. 'Moi, camarade ... pas enemie, pas enemie' – bridging nationalism
and hatred in *Westfront 1918* (1930) (BFI Stills, Posters and Designs)

tion, dully resigned to their fate. ... No memorial tells of their
suffering; and words fly like leaves on the wind. Over the bodies
of ten million slain, life goes its accustomed way.'[25]

The film is a faithful re-creation of the book. It is the last year
of the war. German soldiers are billeted in a French house behind
the German lines. There, the student (Hans Joachim Moebius),
the Bavarian (Fritz Kampers) and Karl (Gustav Diessl) flirt with
Yvette (Jackie Monnier), who shares the house with her grand-
father. Whilst the household shelters from artillery attack, Yvette
and the student realise that they are in love, but he leaves soon
after when they are mobilised.

They are led to the front by the lieutenant (Claus Clausen).
Once again they face artillery attack, this time from their own
forces. Karl and the Bavarian are trapped underground and
struggle desperately to shore up their collapsing dug-out. The

student is sent to call off the attack; on his way he finds the smouldering, dead body of a dog sent before him.

The two soldiers are rescued from the dug-out. The student gets the attack called off. At headquarters he sees how plentiful the food is. On his way to visit Yvette he passes groups of men making many wooden crosses. After seeing his lover he returns to the front. He meets Karl, who is on leave for the first time in eighteen months, and tells him of his love for Yvette. Karl is not so lucky. He reaches home as more troops are being mobilised for the front and, after giving short shrift to a fat businessman who questions the failure to take Paris, he discovers his wife in bed with the butcher's son. He threatens him at gunpoint, and demands that they kiss, before throwing him out. Karl's mother, in the meantime, arrives home after a failed mission to buy meat. Karl returns to the front without reconciliation.

The attack is now on. The student is killed during brutal hand-to-hand combat, and Yvette's home is destroyed (she is reluctant to leave as her lover will not be able to find her). Karl and the Bavarian volunteer for a mission, though suicidal, and, after a lengthy battle, the Bavarian is killed and Karl is injured fatally. As he lies in hospital, the lieutenant, now insane, is carried in. As the French soldier in the next bed grasps the hand of the now dead Karl, he says: 'Moi, camarade ... pas enemie, pas enemie' – 'Me comrade ... not enemy, not enemy.' Pabst's closing message, *Ende?!* is expressed in huge letters, showing that he hoped, but doubted, that this was, in fact, the end of war.

Westfront 1918 is an important film, but slow in parts and, although there may be verisimilitude in the combat scenes, one of these is far too long to retain interest. Nevertheless, there remain moments of considerable power. The film conveyed the traditional anti-war messages about the brutality of conflict, the suffering of those at the front and at home, the futility of it all. There are traditional motifs: the queues for meat, the good food enjoyed by the High Command, the masses of wooden crosses, and the cathedral used as a hospital.

War is undoubtedly hell – on the battlefield and off. On the battlefield, death is the only certainty, whether it is from artillery, combat, mechanised warfare or grenade. All the leads die, apart from the lieutenant who is driven mad. The scene in the trench where he is hit is one of the most memorable in war films, and that of his rapid descent into madness one of the most powerful and disturbing.

One reason for *Westfront 1918* being little known is that an English-language version was never prepared (this makes the initial critical success of the film all the more remarkable). Audiences had to watch it either with a few subtitles, or with a commentary. It is an unjustly neglected film because of this, and a fully subtitled version should be prepared.

Important films followed, and two have become classics: Jean Renoir's *La Grande Illusion* (1937) and *Paths of Glory* (1957), Stanley Kubrick's quintessential study of military incompetence and the brutality it engenders. Both were controversial, and were banned in some countries, which showed that the Great War – by the time of the release of Kubrick's film this had become the *First* World War – continued to have a hold on the popular imagination and on international politics. These two, and *All Quiet on the Western Front*, are the three films which need to be seen by anyone interested in anti-war cinema and the Myth.

Two of these films were based on classic novels. Humphrey Cobb's *Paths of Glory* was published in 1935 (it was Cobb's only book). It missed the classic phase of anti-war literature and, despite a number of attempts, was not filmed for another twenty-two years. Based on a true story, it is a bitter and acerbic view, though written with great style. Conversely, *All Quiet on the Western Front* is more famous: Erich Maria Remarque had crafted a spare, telling story, one whose condemnation of the war was total, even if understated (at least by the men who feature in the narrative). Remarque, and his book, are the subjects of Chapter 2.

2

Erich Maria Remarque and
All Quiet on the Western Front

The film of *All Quiet on the Western Front* was based on the novel *Im Westen nichts Neues* by Erich Maria Remarque, first published in 1929 in Germany and then rapidly translated and published worldwide. Although works of disillusionment with the war had appeared before, Remarque's book was a bombshell. Of the hundreds of books published about the war it was the one read most widely, and the one most influential in laying the foundations for a new view of the war as brutal, pointless waste. The impact of this should not be underestimated: during the war propaganda was one-way, and even those who had fought at the front had been reluctant to let their loved ones hear the truth (those who tried were often censored). In a poem written in 1917, though not published then, Gilbert Frankau commented on the wartime view of war books:

> About your book, I've read it carefully,
>   So has Macfaddyen; (You remember him,
> the light-haired chap who joined us after Loos?)
>   And candidly we don't think much of it.
>
>   My grief, but we're fed up to the back teeth
> with war-books, war-verse, all the eye-wash stuff

8. Carl Laemmle, founder of Universal Pictures, and Erich Maria Remarque, author of *All Quite on the Western Front* (author's collection)

that seems to please the idiots at home.
You know the kind of thing, or used to know:
'Heroes who laugh while Fritz is strafing them'
(I don't remember that *you* found it fun
The day they shelled us out of Blauwpoort Farm!)

You *have* forgotten, or you couldn't write
this sort of stuff, all cant, no guts in it,
hardly a single picture true to life.

Lord, if I'd half your brains I'd write a book:
None of your sentimental platitudes,
but something real, vital, that should strip
the glamour from this outrage we call war,
showing it naked, hideous, stupid, vile –
one vast abomination …

It was many years before the glamour of war could be stripped away. Although the bitter poetry of the war had first been published before 1918, ten years had passed before the anti-war prose appeared. Distance was needed before those who had fought could bring themselves to re-create the horror and brutality of the trenches. Samuel Hynes said that for 'a period of nearly a decade, there was a curious imaginative silence about the greatest occurrence of recent history.'[1] Edmund Blunden, whose *Undertones of War* (1928) was one of the first realist portrayals, had tried to write after the war but found it too painful. He said:

> Why should I not write it?
>
> I know that the experience to be sketched in it is very local, limited, incoherent; that it is almost useless, in the sense that no one will read it who is not already aware of all the intimations and discoveries in it, and many more, by reason of having gone the same journey. No one? Some, I am sure; but not many. *Neither will they understand* – that will not be all my fault.[2]

He was not the only one. Richard Aldington, in a review of *In Retreat* by Herbert Read, wrote: 'Those who have attempted to convey any real war experience, sincerely, unsentimentally, avoiding ready-made attitudes (pseudo-heroic or pacifist or quasi-humorous), must have felt the torturing sense of something incommunicable ... It wasn't a question of anyone's being brave; it was a question of trying to communicate the incommunicable.'[3] According to Modris Eksteins, T. E. Lawrence had agreed with Robert Graves that the war would never be mentioned when they spoke, and this was the wider public view: Ilya Ehrenburg recorded that in Berlin in 1921: 'The artificial limbs of war-cripples did not creak, empty sleeves were pinned up with safety-pins. Men whose faces had been scorched by flame-throwers wore large black spectacles. The lost war took care to camouflage itself as it roamed the streets.'[4]

The situation had changed by the end of the decade.

Remarque's book was one of many published between 1928 and 1932 about the war. All contained a realistic view of trench combat showing the futility and brutality of conflict; all fulfilled the myth of the war: in 1928 *Undertones of War* and Arnold Zweig's *The Case of Sergeant Grischa*; in 1929 R. C. Sherriff's *Journey's End* (the play, though a novelisation was published in 1930), Richard Aldington's *Death of a Hero*, Robert Graves's *Goodbye to All That*, and Ernest Hemingway's *A Farewell to Arms*; in 1930 Frederic Manning's *Her Privates We* and Henry Williamson's *The Patriot's Progress*; in 1931 Wilfred Owen's collected poetry and, in 1933, Vera Brittain's *Testament of Youth*.

Remarque's book was also a masterwork. Like the film that followed, it was highly controversial, particularly in the author's homeland. It was a bestseller from publication day and, unlike many of its contemporaries (though not those noted above), has rarely been out of print since then. The *Nouvelles littéraires* called him in October 1930 'the author today with the largest audience in the world'.[5] After being rejected by leading German publishers, it was published by Ullstein, a Jewish company (which gave an added weapon to the Nazis' campaign against the book, film and author).

A clever marketing campaign made the publication an event, and, following serialisation in the *Vossische Zeitung* for two months at the end of 1928 (the newspaper sold out each issue), it was published triumphantly on the last day of January, 1929. The whole tone of the marketing was summed up in the announcement by the *Vossische Zeitung* of the serialisation: 'Erich Maria Remarque, not a professional author, a young man in his early thirties, has suddenly, just a few months ago, found the need, the urge to put into words that which befell him and his school friends, an entire class of young, life-loving men of whom not a single one survived.'[6]

The numbers in print, in a very short time, were remarkable: within three months over 600,000 copies had been sold, foreign translations had been made rapidly and it was a key choice of the

American Book of the Month Club. Within fifteen months, over two-and-a-half million copies were in print worldwide. An advertisement in the *New York Times* in May 1930 by the publishers, Little, Brown, tied to the film's release, highlights the extent to which *All Quiet on the Western Front* had impressed an international audience with its sales. The following had been sold:[7]

Germany	999,000
France	440,000
England	310,000
America	335,000
Sweden	66,000
Denmark/Norway	70,000
Hungary	28,000
Spain	75,000
Holland	65,000
Finland	22,000
Russia	60,000
Japan	45,000

In all, there were twenty translations in print by this time (it was eventually to appear in Afrikaans, Chinese, Croat, Danish, Esperanto, Finnish, Hebrew (in Warsaw), Icelandic, Macedonian, Russian, Tamil, Urdu and Yiddish, amongst many other translations). A Braille copy was sent free of charge to all blind veterans in Germany who requested a copy. Ullstein was so impressed with sales that they gave Remarque a Lancia car.

Such sales figures were extraordinary: that millions of people were flocking to buy a *war* book at a time when publishing was in recession made it all the more remarkable. The downside was that publishers rushed into print all manner of war literature. In Germany, Emil Marius Requark (*sic*) wrote *Vor Troja nichts Neues*, a 'feeble skit', according to Modris Eksteins, on Remarque's work, though one which sold 20,000 copies.[8] A publisher in Britain jumped on the bandwagon with Helen Zenna Smith's story of women ambulance drivers, *'Not So Quiet ... ': Stepdaughters of War*, which had three quick editions, a French translation, was staged as a play and was reprinted again in the 1980s by a British feminist publisher (there was also a sequel in 1931, *Women of the Aftermath*).[9]

Remarque's book was praised widely, at home and internationally, though its publication attracted much criticism. Over two hundred articles and essays appeared about the book in Germany in 1929; the controversy was such that Ullstein issued a pamphlet examining arguments for and against the book, *Der Kampf um Remarque* (*The Battle Around Remarque*). Walter von Molo, the president of the German Academy of Letters, said: 'Let this book into every home that has suffered no loss in the War, and to every home that had to sacrifice any of its kindred, for these are the words of the dead, the testament of all the fallen, addressed to the living of all nations.'[10] Joseph Goebbels provided a different view: in his diary he condemned Remarque as a 'draftee' and called his book corrupting and mean-spirited.[11]

The English-language version was translated by Arthur Wesley Wheen (known as A. W. Wheen).[12] Considering that he had brought Remarque's prose to millions of readers – as he was later to do with his translation of Remarque's other books, *The Road Back* and *Three Comrades*; he also translated Johannsen's *Four Infantrymen on the Western Front, 1918* – little is known of Wheen. After translating *Three Comrades*, he seems to have disappeared without trace. He did publish one story in 1929 with Faber and Faber in their *Criterion Miscellany* (a First World War piece, written originally in 1923), but nothing more is known about his life. Wheen's translation lasted sixty-four years, and it is regarded as poor and sometimes inaccurate. A new edition, translated by Brian Murdoch and published in 1994, is definitive.[13]

What Wheen did give, and for this he is owed eternal gratitude, is the title. Remarque's original German title, translated as *Nothing New on the Western Front*, is turned into *All Quiet on the Western Front*. Whilst the original is clever, pointing out that death is normal and that one death is not worth a report, Wheen's is memorable, almost poetic, and has entered the language. It may not, however, be original: Brian Murdoch points out that Wheen possibly adapted it from a song from the American Civil War, 'All Quiet along the Potomac' by Ethel Lynn Beers, about the failure to report a soldier's death.

A number of cuts were made to the English translation by Putnam in Britain and Little, Brown in America, which removed some of the scatology, obscenity and licentiousness (particular targets included descriptions of bodily functions and a sex scene in the hospital). The scene where the men talk whilst sitting on latrines survived in Britain (it was deleted in America following representations by the Book of the Month Club), though some critics accused Remarque of being a filthy and dirty novelist. An editorial in the *London Mercury* stated: '"Criticism", wrote Anatole France, "is the adventure of the soul among masterpieces." The adventure of the soul among lavatories is not inviting; but this, roughly, is what criticism of recent translated German novels must be ... The modern Germans ... suppose that lavatories are intensely interesting. They are obsessed by this dreary subject, and they are obsessed by brutality.'[14]

The fact that this was not a full version failed to have an impact on sales in Britain and America (few would, in actual fact, have known, and, as Remarque spoke no English, he would not have been in a position to comment). In Britain, Herbert Read, a war veteran, said it had 'swept like a gospel over Germany' and called it 'the first completely satisfying expression in literature of the greatest event of our time'. He had read it six times by this stage. It clearly had resonance for Read: like Remarque, he knew that the end of the war was just the beginning of the futile search for meaning. He wrote:

> No idealism is left in this generation. We cannot believe in democracy, or Socialism, or the League of Nations. To be told at the front that we were fighting to make the world safe for democracy was to be driven to the dumb verge of insanity. On a mutual respect for each other's sufferings we

built up that sense of comradeship which was the war's only good gift. But death destroyed even this, and we were left with only the bare desire to live, although life itself was past our comprehension.[15]

H. G. Wells was also impressed. 'It's wonderful,' he said.[16] Lowes Dickinson, in the *Cambridge Review*, said that readers should not fear German propaganda: 'The book is far above all that. It is the truth, told by a man with the power of a great artist, who is hardly aware what an artist he is.'[17] And the London *Times* said that the book 'possesses characteristics of genius beyond any nationalism'.[18]

Not all in Britain liked the book. In a remarkable article by J. C. Squire in the *London Mercury*, Remarque – and, by implication, all Germans – were accused of dissembling:

We repeat ... (being cosmopolitans and pacifists, but facers of facts) that the Germans (many of whom were not even Christianized until the sixteenth century) have contributed very little indeed to European culture ... In war we exaggerated the defects of the enemy; do not let us, in peace, exaggerate his merits; above all, do not let us, in a wanton reaction, take more interest in the enemy than in the friend ... Peace with the Germans, by all means; understanding with the Germans, if possible; but let us not out of mere sentimentality, concentrate our gaze upon the Germans at the expense of more cultivated, productive and civilized peoples.[19]

In France, Remarque's book was part of an extensive range of war literature: by 1928, 303 books by 252 authors had been published. Indeed, the first anti-war book had appeared in France in 1916: Henri Barbusse's *Le Feu* was an instant success, winning the Prix Goncourt in 1917 and selling 300,000 copies by 1918. Remarque's book was just as successful. One critic said that the huge sales were 'a sort of plebiscite in favor of peace. Every volume bought is equivalent to a vote.'[20] Within ten days of publication, *All Quiet on the Western Front* had sold 72,000 copies, and by the end of 1929 around 450,000.

The book was also received well in the United States. Frank B. Kellogg, a former secretary of state, said that it was 'certainly a remarkable book'.[21] H. L. Mencken called it a 'gorgeous and epical paean to the indomitable spirit of youth. Unquestionably the best story of the World War so far published.'[22] The reviewer in *The Chicago Tribune* said that he 'couldn't put it down. It's the realest, most terrifying, most gripping novel of the war we've ever read,'[23] and Frank Ernest Hill in the New York *Herald Tribune* said it was 'obviously founded on indelible fact, and might be an authentic autobiographical account'.[24] By the end of August 1929, sixty-four newspapers – from the *Beacon Journal* in Akron, Ohio to the *Republican-Herald* in Winona, Minnesota – had carried serialisations of the novel.

Even those in the High Command – easy, and often justifiable, targets in anti-war literature – were forced to admit that there was something in what Remarque had said. General James A. Drain, the former National Commander of the American Legion, said: 'The genius of the German soldier author brings the essence of the war closer to the mind and soul than anything else in literature, sculpture or painting.'[25] Sir Ian Hamilton, the commanding general at the disastrous Gallipoli campaign, in a generous review for *Life and Letters*, said: 'There was a time when I would have strenuously combated Remarque's inferences and conclusions':

> Now, sorrowfully, I must admit, there is a great deal of truth in them. Latrines, rats, lice; smells, blood, corpses; scenes of sheer horror as where comrades surround the deathbed of a young *Kamerad* with one eye on his agonies, the other on his new English boots; the uninspired strategy; the feeling that the leaders are unsympathetic or stupid; the shrivelling up of thought and enthusiasm under ever-growing machinery of an attrition war; all this lasting too long – so long indeed that half a million souls, still existing in our own island, have

been, in Remarque's own terrible word, 'lost'. Why else, may I ask, should those who were once the flower of our youth form to-day so disproportionate a number of the down and out?[26]

Hamilton was not so generous as to agree with all that Remarque had written – he went on, for example, to talk about the good that came out of the war – but he had conceded, one felt. He also managed to coax Remarque out of his self-imposed silence, as he felt that Hamilton was the only person up to then who had understood what he was trying to convey (as with his book, Remarque's letters were translated by Wheen):

> my work … was not political, neither pacifist nor militarist, in intention, but human simply. It presents the war as seen within the small compass of the front-line soldier, pieced together out of many separate situations, out of minutes and hours, out of struggle, fear, dirt, bravery, dire necessity, death and comradeship … from which the word Patriotism is only *seemingly* absent, because the simple soldier never spoke of it. His patriotism lay in the *deed* (not in the *word*); it consisted simply in the fact of his presence at the front. For him that was enough. He cursed and swore at the war; but he fought on, and fought on even when already without hope.[27]

He went on:

> I merely wanted to awaken understanding for a generation that more than all others has found it difficult to make its way back from the four years of death, struggle and terror, to the peaceful fields of work and progress. Thousands upon thousands have even yet been unable to do it.[28]

The success of the book created many problems in addition to the deletions made in Britain and the USA. Remarque was denounced as a Marxist pacifist and his book was banned in military libraries in Czechoslovakia in November 1929, and in

1930 in schools in Thuringia in central Germany by the minister for education (and Nazi), Dr Wilhelm Frick – 'It is time to stop the infection of the schools with pacifist propaganda,' he said.[29]

Worse was to come. *All Quiet on the Western Front* joined the ranks of other great humanitarian works in the Nazi book-burnings on 10 May 1933. Goebbels, Hitler's spokesman, read out the names of the condemned authors to the crowd. A Nazi student cried: 'Down with the literary betrayal of the soldiers of the world war! In the name of educating our people in the spirit of valour, I commit the writings of Erich Maria Remarque to the flames.'[30] Just over six months later, copies were seized by the police 'for the protection of the German people', as the 4 February presidential decree stated, and these were destroyed the following month. By this stage Remarque had already been forced into exile. On the night of the burnings, he was in Ascona, drinking with the author Emil Ludwig. Ludwig said later, 'We opened our oldest Rhine wine, turned on the radio, heard the flames crackling, heard the speeches of the Hitler spokesman – and drank to the future.'[31] Ironically, two storm-troopers spent the time guarding Remarque's agent, Otto Klement, and, bored, they read *All Quiet on the Western Front* and *The Road Back*.[32]

Remarque was born Erich Paul Remark on 22 June 1898 (it has often been said, and was a point made particularly by the Nazis, that Remark was originally born Kramer and reversed the spelling when he became successful).[33] His childhood was disrupted (the family moved home many times to keep rent payments low), but he showed early promise as a writer – he was so good, in fact, that one teacher accused him of plagiarism – and was popular with other boys. A tender, bookish boy, who read widely in the works of Herman Hesse, Jack London, Dostoevsky and Rilke, amongst many others, he was often prone to suicidal feelings. He wanted to be a writer or a musician.

In 1916 he joined the Circle of the Träumbude, the Dream Circle, whose leader, Friedrich Hörstemeier, became a father figure and was hugely influential in his development (Remark had always got on better with his mother than with his father). The Circle were free spirits, devoted to nudity and sexual freedom, and had an aim of transforming Osnabrück into a cultural city like Dresden and Berlin. They met to discuss their work and to attack authority. The war interrupted this Bohemian, bucolic idyll. Remarque said in 1930: '[At seventeen] I was dreaming that I should become a composer, and behold, I found myself thrown into barracks and then, a few weeks later, I was sent to the front. My life had changed the moment when I began to organize it freely in accordance with my dreams.'[34]

Although critics and enemies accused him of having fabricated his military experience, Remarque was undoubtedly a veteran, and the war had a great influence on him, though not perhaps to the extent which some reviewers had suggested. *All Quiet on the Western Front* was certainly not autobiography, though it, and his other books, contained autobiographical sections. What his army life did provide him with − and this is true for his schooldays, and his whole life, effectively − was essential material for his books, including some of the key characters: his best friend at school became Kemmerich; Konschorek, a staff member, was the basis for Kantorek; Himmelreich, who conducted drill at the recruit training camp, became Himmelstoss, the hated drill sergeant. Even his mother's cancer (she died during the war) and his own butterfly collection appeared.

As a pacifist he had resisted enlistment as long as possible. During his period in the army, he never actually reached the front, although he was wounded seriously enough to have to spend fifteen months in hospital. There he became opposed to the war, and to German society, and felt that the one positive thing to emerge from the war would be that German youth would discover themselves. He was found fit for active duty at the end of October 1918 but did not travel to the front before the Armistice.

Like many of his veteran friends, he found it hard to return to life in a defeated and humiliated Germany. Hanns-Gerd Rabe, a friend of Remarque's, commented on the spirit of the time: 'I had just handed over my plane to the English and arrived at the train station in Osnabrück. The properly attired station attendant demanded that I surrender my travel ticket. I begged his forgiveness for having returned home alive from the war. Unfortunately no train tickets were sold during the war, only one-way tickets for a hero's death.'[35] Harley U. Taylor Jr said: 'It was to this volatile and vitriolic situation that Remarque and his comrades returned. ... Remarque, who placed a very high value on comradeship, was appalled by the sight of former comrades who had survived the horrors of the war now opposing each other in combat ... Adjustment to civilian life was not easy for Remarque and his friends.'[36] Remarque himself commented:

> Our generation has grown up in a different way from all others before and afterward. Their one great and most important experience was the war. No matter whether they approved or rejected it; whether they understood it from a nationalistic, pacifistic, adventurous, religious, or stoic point of view. They saw blood, horror, annihilation, struggle, and death ... I [have] avoided taking sides from every political, social, religious or other point of view ... I have spoken only of the terror, of the horror, of the desperate, often brutal impulses of self-preservation, of the tenacious hold on life, face to face with death and annihilation.[37]

The Road Back was influenced strongly by his own experiences, and those of his friends, members of this lost generation. The mood of the time, and the political use to which it was put by the Right, is summed up in the Nazi marching-cry 'The Song of the Lost Troops':[38]

> Remember that hour heavy with gloom,
> Germany sinking to Communist doom,
> Germany abandoned, betrayed, despised,

Street and square with blood baptized:
Don't you remember?

Remarque was affected mentally by the war as well as being physically wounded. At home he began to wear medals he had not been awarded, and uniforms above his rank. Later, he purchased a title. Remarque researcher Thomas Schneider said he needed recognition after all he had been through:

> He was very young and he'd lost everything – his mother, his mentor – so he had to find a place again in the society. He had no bright vision of his future at that time, so he needed a symbol, and perhaps tried to find his identity by these acts, or by this 'acting.' He also wore a monocle. And the people in the small town of Osnabrück would say, 'Look, there is that Remark kid. He's really foolish.' But they would talk about him; they'd give him recognition, which he badly needed. ... So, he got himself an image in a way.[39]

Remarque wrote *All Quiet on the Western Front* to expiate the malaise and depression which had afflicted him and his friends since 1918. It had taken him nine years to identify the war as the cause of his despair. Just after the publication of his book he commented:

> I suffered from rather violent attacks of despair. When attempting to overcome these attacks, it happened that gradually, with full consciousness and systematically, I began to look for the cause of my depressions; in consequence of this intentional analysis my mind reverted to my experiences during the war. I was able to observe quite similar phenomena in my acquaintances and friends. We all were – and are often to the present day the victims of restlessness; we lack a final object; at times we are supersensitive, at times indifferent but over and above all we are bereft of any joy. The shadows of the war oppressed us, and particularly so when

we did not think of it at all. On the very day on which these ideas swept over me, I began to write.[40]

In the interim, he had been employed as a teacher, a writer (of poetry and prose), a tombstone salesman, an organist in a mental asylum in Osnabrück, and an editor of *Sport im Bild* magazine. In the midst of all this he had married, and completed two novels. The first, *Die Träumbude* (*The Dream Room*) was published in 1920. It was not well received and disappeared without trace, and the success of *All Quiet on the Western Front* prompted Ullstein to purchase any surviving copies. The second, *Station am Horizont* (*Station on the Horizon*), a story about racing drivers, was published in eight issues of *Sport im Bild*. Again it disappeared, though material from it was used later in his novel *Heaven Has No Favorites* (1961).

Writing in the evenings, he completed *All Quiet on the Western Front* within six weeks. He did not submit it for publication immediately, however, preferring to leave it for six months. He gave it first to Fischer Verlag, one of Germany's leading publishers, who rejected it as they felt war books were not commercial. A friend, Curt Riess, told Remarque he was not surprised: 'Who, today, ten years after the end of the war, wants to know anything about the war? I would tear up the manuscript, throw it away, and forget about it.'[41] Another acquaintance, Billy Wilder, the film director, also encouraged Remarque to pack the whole thing in – not only was he facing failure with a book no one would be interested in, but he was sacrificing a well-paid job:

I knew Remarque quite well. He was the editor of a magazine which was sort of the equivalent of *Vogue* magazine … He had the plushest, most esteemed job you could have gotten in German journalism. I was a reporter and writer back then. We had lunch here and there, and one day at one of those lunches, he told me that incredible idea of his. He was going to quit his job and finish his novel. And I thought he was just absolutely out of his mind. 'Who wants to quit this job?

I mean, you can't go any higher!' He said, 'Well, my wife insisted I finish the book.' I said: 'What is it about?' He said: 'It's about World War I.' And I said: 'My God, now!?! This is 1928. Who is interested in the world war?' ... And I'm sure that other friends of his – colleagues – had tried to talk him out of taking ... what we then thought [the] suicidal move of giving up a great career.[42]

Despite the success of the novel, and subsequently the film, *All Quiet on the Western Front* was not to provide the catharsis Remarque yearned for, and he never escaped the war. He completed a trilogy of First World War books with *The Road Back* (1931) and *Three Comrades* (1937), both of which were filmed. Much of his work after this was concerned with Nazism and the Second World War, and many of these books were also filmed: *So Ends Our Night* (based on *Flotsam*, 1947), *Arch of Triumph* (1948, directed by Lewis Milestone), *A Time to Love and a Time to Die* (1958), amongst others.

As well as forcing him out of his homeland and burning his books, the Nazis took further revenge later when they executed his sister, Elfriede Scholz, *née* Remark, in December 1943 for defeatism, and for attacking the Führer. She was beheaded. The fact that she was the brother of the despised Erich Maria Remarque was not lost on the court – at one point the president said: 'Your brother, unfortunately, got away. But you are not going to get away.'[43] Someone who knew her told Remarque three years after the war that she behaved with great dignity and courage, even refusing to stand and make the Nazi salute in the court room.

Remarque was nominated for the Nobel Peace Prize in 1931 by Dr Sigismond Cybichowski, professor of state and people's law at the University of Warsaw and member of the Permanent Court of Justice in the Hague. This was not the first time it had been proposed that Remarque receive the accolade. He had been nominated in 1929, but this had been opposed by the German

Officers' Association: they said that the success of his book was more to do with a clever publicity campaign than with the truth well told, and that Remarque had misled and insulted readers, indeed all Germans, with his claims about his wartime service.

Cybichowski said that Remarque had promoted the cause of peace with *All Quiet on the Western Front*, but offered no further evidence to support his case. As with all nominations from those eligible to put proposals forward, the Norwegian Parliamentary Nobel Committee prepared a detailed report. This cleared Remarque of the accusation that it had all been a publicity ploy:

> The enormous, indeed unique success cannot, of course, be due to Ullstein's advertising and the polemics over it ... It must be that the book satisfies a need, that its portrayal of war corresponds to the masses' impressions of it. It stands alongside Barbusse's *Le Feu* as the war novel *par excellence*. ... It is undeniably a creative work by a person who has lived through the horrors and disillusionment of war. It contains lifelike, indeed gripping portraits from the front, full of striking observations. The visit home, with the contrasting atmospheres of the army and the home, is excellently done from an artistic point of view.[44]

However, it concluded that, in spite of its qualities, which were great, the book was 'not well composed' and was too negative to serve the cause of peace:

> The point is not just to scare people away from war, but to create a new atmosphere, a new public opinion. This can only be done by encouraging the broad masses to work actively for peace, teaching them about foreign people's views, showing them how conflicts can be resolved and war be avoided, encouraging them to see each nation's interest in a world community, in peaceful productive cooperation – i.e. moral disarmament and organisation.[45]

The nomination made no further progress. The Nobel Peace

Prize that year was awarded jointly to Jane Addams, the veteran American peace campaigner, and Nicholas Murray Butler, president of Columbia University and promoter of the Kellogg–Briand pact (in addition to Remarque, Cybichowski had also nominated Butler).

In late January 1933, Remarque was warned by a friend to get out of Germany quickly. He left at once for Switzerland. He was not to return to Germany until 1952, the year that *All Quiet on the Western Front* was shown again on the German screen. 'In the year 1933 I had to leave Germany because my life was threatened,' he said. 'I was neither a Jew nor oriented toward the left politically. ... I was a militant pacifist. ... It's more by luck than good judgment that I am on the side I now stand on. But I know that it happens to be the right one.'[46]

By this time, *All Quiet on the Western Front* as a film had caused as much controversy as his book. Remarque had little to do with the film (he had only a minor involvement in most of the films of his work). This was left to a group of people, many of whom became known as 'the Boys of *All Quiet*'. The boys, and the others involved in the production of the film, are covered in the next chapter.

3

The 'Boys of *All Quiet*'

T he view that film is the most collaborative of the arts is exemplified by the remarkable team that came together to make *All Quiet on the Western Front* – 'The Boys of *All Quiet*',[1] as William Bakewell called the actors and technical staff. Many of them were new to motion pictures, or relative novices; some became lifelong friends; one was to become a star; a few were influenced profoundly by the film's message. This proved to be one of those happy experiences where all those involved combine to create a great work of art, as well as classic entertainment.

There was more to *All Quiet on the Western Front* than Bakewell's boys, however. The production brought together some of the best talent Hollywood and Broadway could offer in writing, acting, direction and production. Heading all this was the remarkable Carl Laemmle, president and company founder of Universal Pictures, and his son Carl Laemmle Junior, who in April 1929 had been made head of production as, it is said, a twenty-first birthday present. Hollywood lore has it that Laemmle was a nepotistic employer (according to Norman Zierold, at the time of the disposal of the studio over seventy relatives, pensioners and friends of relatives were on the books[2]), leading to the oft-quoted rhyme, 'Uncle Carl Laemmle/Has a very large faemmle.' The attribution of this to Ogden Nash is disputed, however.

Carl Laemmle personified the American dream. Although he

9. The 'Boys of *All Quiet*' – and one woman! (author's collection)

rose from humble beginnings to become one of the great figures of Hollywood history, he is not as widely known as other moguls. One problem may be that of all the great producers, Laemmle was – as Neal Gabler says in *An Empire of Their Own*, his book on the Hollywood Jewish producers – the most improbable: 'He looked like an avuncular elf – five feet two inches tall, a constant gap-toothed smile, merry little eyes, a widening expanse of pate, and a slight paunch that was evidence of the beer and the food he enjoyed.'[3] He was generous and liked by all, in an industry and at a time when such attitudes were eschewed.

His rise followed a route similar to that of some other moguls. Born Jewish in Germany in 1867, he moved to America in 1884, where he was employed in a number of clerical jobs, as an errand boy and a farmhand before opening a Nickelodeon theatre in 1906 in Chicago. He had wanted to buy a clothes or a five-and-dime store (he had owned a clothing store previously, in 1903 in Oshkosh, Winsconsin), but one wet night he visited a 'hole-in-the-wall five-cent motion picture theater':

> The pictures made me laugh, though they were very short and the projection jumpy. I liked them, and so did everybody else. I knew right away that I wanted to go into the motion picture business. ... 'Funny pictures are the thing,' I said to myself. 'Charge people and make them laugh.' Everybody wants to laugh. ... As I walked back to my hotel that night in Chicago, I began to build my plans, and the next day I learned everything I possibly could about the business. Three weeks after watching those funny pictures ... I owned my own theater.[4]

This was The White Front – so called to symbolise cleanliness and purity and so to offset the concerns of American reformers at the time about the effect moving pictures were having on society.

Laemmle's rise was swift, helped by the massive growth of the industry at the time and the development of the audience (and his skills as a self-publicist): a chain of movie houses; his own distribution company (the Laemmle Film Service); victor in 1912 – in a bitter, three-year battle – over Thomas Edison's attempt to create a monopoly in the industry; founder of Universal Pictures (based on, he said, the fact that they were providing 'universal entertainment for the universe', though the name itself came to Laemmle when he saw a truck for Universal Pipe Fittings pass by); architect of Universal City, the best studio of the time when it opened in 1915.

By 1930 Laemmle had become a pacifist, and he was particularly proud of *All Quiet on the Western Front*. In a speech in May that year, just after the film's release, he said: 'if there was anything in my life I am proud of, it is this picture. It is, to my mind, a picture that will live forever.'[5] He had not always been a pacifist, however. During the war his views followed public opinion. In 1915 he was one of the supporters of Henry Ford's Peace Ship (the ill-fated attempt by the car magnate to end the war). Later he supported American intervention, even though it was against his homeland, and he joined other Hollywood producers in making pro-war films, including the notorious 1918 release, *The Kaiser: The Beast of Berlin*. In the mid-1920s he was an enthusiastic advocate and financial supporter of the campaign to send relief to Germany, in particular his birthplace, Laupheim, where the burghers were so struck by his generosity that they named a street after him.

Neither Laemmle nor Milestone was nominated for the Nobel Peace Prize, unlike Remarque. To try to advance his case, Laemmle commissioned an official biography from the English dramatist John Drinkwater.[6] This was no critical study (and, unfortunately, it is the only biography of Laemmle). Drinkwater quoted approvingly the writer Kenneth C. Burton: 'And why, therefore, should not Carl Laemmle have the Nobel Peace Prize? ... Rightly they may ask what Roosevelt or Root or Wilson and any of the rest of the foreign gentlemen or of the peace societies who have been awarded the prize, ever did more for the peace of the world than Carl Laemmle has with *Western Front*.'[7] Perhaps realising the

10. Carl Laemmle Junior, Universal's Head of Production, and the producer of *All Quiet on the Western Front* (BFI Stills, Posters and Designs)

hopelessness of such a claim, he suggested that Remarque, Milestone and Laemmle should be awarded the prize jointly.

It was Laemmle's background that led the left-wing critic, Harry

Alan Potamkin, to comment cynically on his prospects: 'Carl Laemmle was suggested for the Nobel Peace Prize for *All Quiet*. During the war he made *The Kaiser, Beast of Berlin*, after the war he wept upon the plight of his *Vaterland* in his advertising column in the *Saturday Evening Post*, and after *All Quiet* he issues a series of sergeant–private–girl farces in which one of the agonized Germans of *All Quiet* is starred. Well, he still qualifies for the prize; he is no less noble than [ex-President Woodrow] Wilson.'[8]

Laemmle Junior was the producer. He was hugely ambitious, possessing the hunger for greatness for the studio that had characterised the period when Irving Thalberg, Hollywood's *wunderkind*, was in charge. *All Quiet on the Western Front* was, nevertheless, a risk: the book was bleak, it represented the German side of the war, and there was little romance. The prospects looked so poor that industry commentators dubbed the film 'Junior's End', a reflection of the production by a rival studio at the same time of the R. C. Sherriff play, *Journey's End*.

The risk was so high, and the company in such financial trouble, that the Universal Board agreed to veto the production with only the Laemmles voting in favour. Laemmle Junior saw it as the vehicle for his ambitions to move Universal into big-budget features (ambitions which, with the depression, were to create financial difficulties for the studio). It was also the case that a war film well made – such as *The Big Parade* and *Wings* – could capture the imagination and make money. Furthermore, *All Quiet on the Western Front* was based on a book which had become a bestseller and *cause célèbre*.

But their strongest card was that Carl Laemmle believed in the stance the book had taken. In one of his columns in *Universal Weekly* – 'Straight from the Shoulder Talk' – he called Remarque's book 'the talk of the world' with an impact comparable to the anti-slavery novel *Uncle Tom's Cabin*. He went on:

> *Nothing like it has ever been done before. It is not a sermon or a preachment, but a simple record of war in its most intimate close-ups – and its very simplicity and lack of adornment make it all the more*

gripping. ... The world will discuss *All Quiet on the Western Front* for generations to come. It will sink into the consciousness of men and nations. ... Read it regardless of your business interest. Read it, and, once having read it, *I defy you to put it out of your mind. It will start your thoughts flowing in a new direction!*[9]

Like his son he was proud of his decision to purchase the book and wanted desperately to make the film. He pushed the decision through. In a profile of Junior in 1934 he said that he considered *All Quiet on the Western Front* 'his greatest achievement, even to this day, after he has made more than three score of excellent pictures'.[10] Such pictures included *Frankenstein*, *Waterloo Bridge* and *The Invisible Man*, which placed the film in good company.

Laemmle chose the Russian-born Lewis Milestone as director of *All Quiet on the Western Front*, although he was not the first choice. Paul Fejos, director of *Lonesome* (a portrayal of leisure activity among working people, released in 1928) and the early musical *Broadway* (1929), claimed to have initiated Laemmle's purchase of the rights for the book and wanted to make the film. He was dropped in favour of Herbert Brenon, whose request for $125,000 Carl Laemmle thought excessive. Brenon made *The Case of Sergeant Grischa* (1930) instead for RKO.

Milestone was the perfect choice. Tired of the strictures sound had brought to motion pictures (this was Milestone's first sound film), and influenced by the great Russian director Eisenstein, he freed the camera, creating some of the most realistic and horrific battle scenes in cinema history. Along the way he earned $5,000 each week, which ultimately (and ironically) cost Universal more than Brenon wanted. He had been born Milstein in Odessa in 1895, brought up in Bessarabia and educated in Germany for a while. He arrived in the United States at the end of 1913 or beginning of 1914 (even Milestone could not remember exactly when), which was fortunate timing, as otherwise he would have ended up a prisoner of war. He volunteered for action, but never went near the front, and ended the war as a veteran of the

11. Lewis Milestone reading *All Quiet on the Western Front* (Wisconsin Center for Film and Theater Research)

Photographic Division of the United States Signal Corps, where he edited army film footage and helped make training films (one had Milestone playing a German soldier). Colleagues included future directors Josef (Von) Sternberg and Wesley Ruggles.

During his time in the Signals Corps he witnessed the impact of war when he had to preserve, photograph and catalogue limbs that had been sent from the battlefield to Washington. He believed that this gave him his feeling for war (he told Kevin Brownlow later that he didn't believe in war and was against violence, but declined to state whether he was a pacifist[11]). He went on to work for Fox and Mack Sennett, with William Seiter at the Ince studios and then Universal. After three films as director, he won an Academy Award for the Great War comedy *Two Arabian Knights* in 1927 (made for Howard Hughes – 'a combination of a drawing-room blithering idiot and an engineering-room genius', Milestone said[12]). Following this he made *The Racket* (1928), again for Hughes, about corruption in the police. The film was nominated for an Academy Award for best picture.

Milestone first encountered *All Quiet on the Western Front* while making *New York Nights* in 1929. Lilyan Tashman, one of the actresses in the film, gave him a copy of the book and told him to read it. He liked it but did not pursue the matter until Herbert Brenon had been rejected. Then Carl Laemmle called him to Universal to discuss the film.

Lewis Milestone was a fiercely independent man, one often at odds with producers, the studios and prevailing opinion (he was one of the Hollywood Nineteen accused by Senator McCarthy of peddling Communist propaganda in their films). He was always proud of *All Quiet on the Western Front*, though he tended 'to resent the fact that my close identification with it has led many to believe it's the only one – or the only one of merit – I ever directed,' as he reflected in 1979.[13]

He has been accused of being inconsistent. It is true that he may have made too many films which he shouldn't have, but even some of his failures had moments of genius. After *All Quiet on the Western Front*, he went on to make such innovative, and always well directed, films as *The Front Page* (1931), *Rain* (1932), *Hallelujah I'm a Bum* (1933), *Of Mice and Men* (1939) and his great, though controversial, story of the Salerno landings in the Second

World War, *A Walk in the Sun* (1946). This film was as brave a piece of film-making as his anti-war classic, and it went much against the grain of films about that war in its portrayal of the routine and boredom of conflict.

The political difficulties of late 1940s and early 1950s America meant that after making *Halls of Montezuma* in 1951, another anti-war film, Milestone was forced to leave Hollywood and the United States to work in Britain and Italy. The poisoned atmosphere in which Milestone lived and worked at this time (he has a large FBI file) is summed up in Hedda Hopper's petty profile of 1948. Hopper was a scabrous gossip columnist. Referring to Milestone's decision to give a job to Ring Lardner Jr, an unfriendly witness in the House UnAmerican Activities Committee hearings, she said:

> Let's take a look at Lardner's new boss. Milestone was born in Chisinau, Russia, and came to this country years ago. He found many friends here. When I first knew him, he was a cutter for Bill Seiter. A man was hired to shake Milestone out of bed each morning so he could get to work on time. He has made some good pictures, and some not so good ... He has a beautiful home, in which he holds leftish rallies, is married to an American, and has made a fortune here. But still his heart seems to yearn for Russia. Wonder if Joe would take him back?[14]

He did not return to the United States until 1957. His last few films were undistinguished affairs, and included the ratpack movie, *Ocean's Eleven* (1960) and the disastrous *Mutiny on the Bounty* with Marlon Brando two years later.

Before the screenplay could be written, the rights had to be secured. Lewis Milestone said the rights were bought by a Herr Friedman, who was in charge of the Universal Exchange in Berlin.[15] He had read the book and thought it would make an excellent film. He borrowed $1,000 and put down an option for the rights. He then told Universal what he had done. Universal records state that the subsequent agreement with Remarque was on a straight percentage basis. However, in his unpublished memoirs, James Bryson – then Universal's managing director, and a man involved in the film industry almost from the start (he had been Carl Laemmle's first business associate) – claimed that he had bought the rights to the film. He paid $25,000, but was told by Laemmle that this was too much. When the popularity of the book became clear, Remarque tried to call the deal off, whilst Laemmle was now keen to secure the rights. He said that Laemmle paid an additional $25,000 later.[16] The final Universal budget for the film (see p. 99) does confirm that $25,000 was allocated, and that the outturn cost was $25,197.19. It does not record whether a further $25,000 was given to Remarque.

Though truncated, and with a straight chronological narrative replacing the flashback structure, the film proved to be a faithful adaptation of the book. The book starts with the episode when the cook refuses to serve the food to the Second Company (this does not appear until the middle of the film). A number of episodes in the book are not in the film (though some are in draft screenplays); these include scenes where animals suffer in war, gas attacks (although this was filmed), Paul Bäumer at training camp (where he encounters some Russian prisoners of war), and the visit of the Kaiser, and it is another character, Franz Wächter (not in the film), who is sent to the dying room.

Some exclusions were made because of the likely objections by censorship offices (they got most of this right, but not all); others simply to ensure that a viable film could be made. Interestingly, the book is more sympathetic to Himmelstoss: whilst he is seen to be a martinet, and they beat him, and he is a coward at the front, he does redeem himself by rescuing one of the boys who is wounded in No Man's Land, and favours them with food. Revenge, however, is exacted upon Kantorek, the teacher. He is enlisted in the Home Guard and has to be drilled by one of his

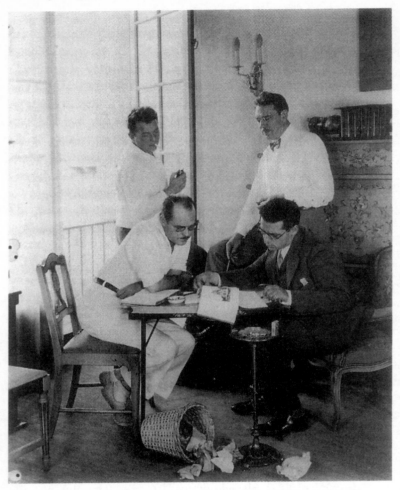

12. The screenwriting team – Lewis Milestone and Maxwell Anderson, standing; Del Andrews and George Cukor, sitting (BFI Stills, Posters and Designs)

ex-pupils who, to motivate him, uses the same words with which he sent them to fight.

The screenwriting team encompassed some of the best talent Hollywood' and Broadway could offer, writers, moreover, who were sympathetic to pacifism. Remarque did claim that Laemmle had asked him to write the screenplay, but he had been advised by his agent to work on *The Road Back* (R. C. Sherriff said that Laemmle had asked him as well). Instead, C. Gardner Sullivan, author of *Civilization*, wrote the original scenario. The final screenplay was written by Del Andrews (editor on *Civilization*), Maxwell Anderson (a pacifist and co-author of *What Price Glory?*) and George Abbott, who was parachuted in from New York to finalise the script.

Bringing the screenplay together was difficult, with Milestone having to intervene directly in the process (eventually, he was to overturn much of Anderson's work). Laemmle Junior had hired Anderson, and had briefed him. For all his playwriting skills, Anderson was not a screenwriter, at least at this stage. When Milestone got hold of Anderson's first attempt, he was horrified: he could not believe that 'the great writer had done something so horrible, so pedestrian and sentimental, so far removed from the spirit of the novel,' as Norman Zierold said.[17] However, he needed a complete draft (Anderson had only provided half by this stage) and sent him away to finish it.

In the meantime, Milestone and his mentor, Del Andrews, who had taught Milestone film-editing and got him a job with the Ince studios, hired a house in Catalina (where they lived next door to John Ford, who expressed grave doubts about the prospects for the film), and set to work. There they dissected the book until they were able to see the framework. They quickly completed the treatment. Anderson finished his own script around a fortnight later and brought it to Milestone, but this was discarded when Anderson read the treatment, and he set to work on turning Andrews' and Milestone's work into the screenplay. There was still a final polish needed, and George Abbott, even then an experienced playwright, was hired. Writing about his role over thirty years later he seemed a little confused:

> Maxwell Anderson had originally been assigned to this task
> but seemed to be having some trouble with the picture tech-

nique or with Junior Laemmle – I never quite understood which – and now they were scheduled to start shooting without a script. I was paid a magnificent salary to rewrite the picture, and when it came out it had one of those baffling credit lines: 'Screen story by George Abbott, Adaptation by Maxwell Anderson, Dialogue by Maxwell Anderson and George Abbott.' I wonder if I fought to get all that. I can't remember.[18]

The role of cinematographer was crucial to the eventual success of the picture. This was still the early sound period and, given the complicated trench scenes, it would be a difficult picture to shoot. Originally slated for the work was Tony Gaudio, who had recently finished *Hell's Angels* and had worked previously on *Two Arabian Nights*. The experience of filming Howard Hughes' epic, however, was enough to put him off war pictures, and he declined.

In the meantime, Universal had heard that Arthur Edeson, the celebrated cinematographer on the silent classics *Robin Hood* and *The Thief of Bagdad*, had made a success of his first sound picture, *In Old Arizona*.[19] Edeson had shot the war picture *The Patent Leather Kid* in 1927 (this was invaluable experience – without this, he doubted if he could have worked on *All Quiet on the Western Front*). The fact that *In Old Arizona* had been shot outdoors, with his specially adapted Mitchell Camera and his 'barney' (a padded bag placed over the camera to keep it quiet), made him all the more likely to succeed with *All Quiet on the Western Front*. After testing the camera for Milestone – and following a review of his material by the whole team – he was given the position at $600 a week. The choice was fully justified when the picture was seen. The realism attained in filming trench combat – the most successful portrayal up to then, and still almost unique – was a great achievement. Edeson went on to become one of the great Hollywood cinematographers, shooting such classic films as *Frankenstein* (1931), *The Invisible Man* (1933), *Sergeant York*, *The Maltese Falcon* (both 1941) and *Casablanca* (1942).

The first roles to be cast were those of Katczinsky, the hard but sympathetic and practical veteran who guides the young recruits in battle, and Himmelstoss, the martinet drill sergeant. Milestone chose Louis Wolheim for Kat. Wolheim had been in an early version of *Dr Jekyll and Mr Hyde* (1920), played in *Two Arabian Knights* for Milestone, and had starred in the stage versions of *The Hairy Ape* and *What Price Glory?* With his broken nose (the result of a football injury), portly figure and rough, booming voice – he was known, rather unkindly, as the ugliest man in Hollywood – Wolheim was ideal. He was also a professor of mathematics with, as William Bakewell said, a 'Fine Arts degree in profanity. His mastery of four-letter words was dazzling ... Sometimes he would deliver them sotto voce, with meticulous articulation, but more often he would bellow them like an erupting volcano.'[20] His fee was $3,500 per week. Wolheim provided the heart of the picture. His portrayal of Katczinsky was perfect, a hard man leavened with humour, and with the right mix of cynicism about the war and empathy with his boys. He died soon after the film was released.

John Wray, a noted Broadway actor recently arrived in Hollywood (he had been appearing in the play *Tin Pan Alley*), was given the part of Himmelstoss, the postman transformed into a sadistic drill sergeant. It was his favourite part, but one destined to be cut heavily on release, as the Germans objected to what they saw as a deliberately misleading portrayal of Teutonic militarism. Less well known than Wolheim, he was paid $1,000 per week. He went on to feature in *I Am a Fugitive from a Chain Gang* (1932) and *The Cat and the Canary* (1939).

It was not such an easy task to fill the other roles, and over two hundred tests were made before the cast was ready. Slim Summerville, former Mack Sennett comedian and an old friend of the director, played the cynical Tjaden (Summerville was the joker on the set; he was also in a comic sketch about *All Quiet on the Western Front* in Paul Whiteman's musical *King of Jazz*, released the same year). Milestone offered him the role when he bumped into him at the Los Angeles Athletic Club. Summerville was keen to break out of comedy roles, but had not yet succeeded so he accepted with alacrity. He was the only one of the cast to feature in the sequel, *The Road Back*, although in the later film the humour with which he had graced *All Quiet on the Western Front* seemed misplaced.

William Bakewell was Albert Kropp, friend of the lead (and Bakewell became a lifelong friend of Lew Ayres, the two having roomed together during production). Bakewell was a Hollywood native and had been 'a wild-eyed movie buff since childhood'.[21] He entered the industry in 1925, playing small parts in a range of films for the studios. *All Quiet on the Western Front* was his seventh sound film.

Ben Alexander, later to feature on television in *Dragnet*, played Kemmerich, whose death in the hospital provides one of the early emotional scenes. Alexander had been a child actor – he played the golden-haired boy in *Hearts of the World* – but had given up the screen to study. After a year at Stanford University, he was home on vacation in Hollywood, where he visited Universal Studios to have lunch with Louis Wolheim. Alexander said in 1940:

> I distinctly remember standing on the set and listening to the familiar sounds: direction; technical talk; camera noises; and arcs humming. Milestone ... came over and said, 'Ben, there's a kid in this story that you could do if you weren't so darn set on being a croaker.' Well, if I had wanted to be a doctor all desire suddenly left me. I knew it was my first love and I've never been frustrated yet in anything I wanted to do so I went back to pictures that day. We worked twenty-three weeks. Worked hard, but none of us realized that the picture would ever really be great.[22]

Smaller roles were played by Scott Kolk (Leer), Owen Davis Jr (Peter), Russell Gleason (Müller – replacing, late in the day,

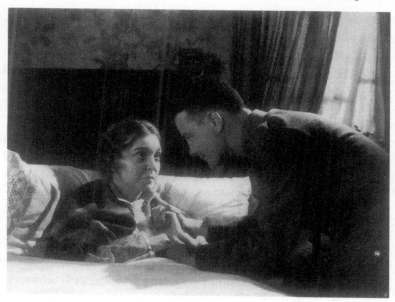

13. Paul Bäumer (Lew Ayres) with Mrs Bäumer (ZaSu Pitts) in a scene
not included in the film because the great actress was replaced by
Beryl Mercer (author's collection)

Allan Lane, who is pictured in some stills) and Walter Browne
Rogers as Behm (though his role was small, he is the one pictured
centrally on all posters and other publicity relating to the film).
The part of Mrs Bäumer was originally played by ZaSu Pitts, but
audience reaction at the preview at San Bernardino – they erupted
with laughter because they had just seen her play in the Paramount
musical, *Honey* – led to her being replaced by Beryl Mercer.
Milestone said that this was probably the only time this would
have happened, but 'the management got scared to death and
said we'd got to replace her ... [as] she is liable to appear in any
number of theatres just before ... showing the picture ... I
couldn't argue with that.'[23]

Mercer was English and some of the team felt this might put
people off, but the part was filmed again (Milestone also took
the opportunity to do some other work on the film). This was a

great shame: although ZaSu Pitts had played a serious role in Erich von Stroheim's film, *Greed*, she had found it hard to break out of comedy. *All Quiet on the Western Front* would have been important for her and, as Bakewell says, she was 'utterly believable in the part, her thin, wan face having the look of a cancer victim'.[24] Marion Clayton, who played Bäumer's sister Erna, was also not the first choice. She replaced Lucille Powers.

For Duval, the French soldier who Bäumer fatally stabs and has to stay with whilst he dies, Milestone cast the great silent comedian and Sennett gag-writer, Raymond Griffith. Griffith had suffered from a vocal affliction since childhood and he could speak only in whispers, but this was not a problem as his role was mainly silent. What *was* a problem was his sense of self-importance: even though his role in *All Quiet on the Western Front* was brief, he wanted his usual rate and, without this, he told Universal that he would rather play the part for no pay. Universal took him at his word![25] This was to be his last screen appearance, one described as 'macabre but telling' by an obituary writer.[26]

At the time, a very different gloss was placed on Griffith's participation. In an interview for *The Picturegoer* published in July 1930 (but done well before this), Milestone recounted the story. This was the hardest scene to film and he was delighted that Griffith, 'with the husky, whispering voice', wanted to play the role:

> Ray Griffith happens to be a great friend of mine, and when he knew I was to do *All Quiet*, he told me he would give anything to appear in the picture, in any sort of part, without his name being mentioned. He is a pacifist, and an enormous admirer of the book; he said he wanted to do what he could for the film, because he thinks the story is such a magnificent argument against war.[27]

He worked hard in the part but received no pay. Milestone said 'He did not receive one cent of money for his work; and his name will not appear on the screen. He would not allow us to put it on; he said: "Let those people who recognise me do so – as for the others, I don't want credit or thanks. If I've been able to help, that's all I care."[28] All that said, Griffith was credited throughout, often fourth behind Wolheim, Ayres and John Wray.

The crucial lead role of Paul Bäumer remained to be cast. Milestone wanted 'a brand new face that nobody ... [had seen] before'.[29] A number of actors were considered, including Douglas Fairbanks Jr, John Wray (who went on to play Himmelstoss), Phillips Holmes (he was to star in Ernst Lubitsch's anti-war classic, *The Man I Killed*, in 1932), Johnny Harron – younger brother of Robert Harron, who had worked with D. W. Griffith in *Hearts of the World* – and even Erich Maria Remarque (he was to feature as an actor in the 1950s film of his book *A Time to Love and a Time to Die*). All were either rejected or unavailable. Fairbanks – surprisingly, as he was well known by 1930 and would not have provided the unknown face the director was after – was favoured by Milestone, but he had other commitments, and United Artists refused to release him (we are probably fortunate that he was unavailable; it seems inconceivable that he would have carried the sensitivity and emotion needed for the role).

It was late in the day when Paul Bern, a producer at MGM and friend of Milestone, suggested Lew Ayres. Ayres had always wanted to be an actor, although he had to settle for being a musician for a while. He failed to break into motion pictures until he had a brief appearance – he spoke one line – in *The Sophomore*, a 1929 picture directed by Leo McCarey (his band, the renowned Henry Halstead Orchestra, also appeared in two Vitaphone shorts for Warner Bros.). He went on to play opposite Greta Garbo in her last silent film, *The Kiss*.

Ayres was keen to be involved with the film, but nearly lost the role that was to make his name. He had already read *All Quiet on the Western Front* a number of times (he was a voracious reader all his life). The story about how he tried to contact Milestone has entered Hollywood legend. Their first conversation was stopped abruptly when Ayres called at 6 a.m., eliciting a curt and crude response; Milestone, who was working nights, was so rude, in fact, that Ayres complained to Bern, who in turn contacted Milestone. This happened again the next day when Ayres called slightly later, although it was still only 7 a.m. Again, Milestone responded angrily.

It was only when he was viewing some test shots which had been made (the film was of the boys at the field kitchen) that he saw the perfect actor for the role: 'I watched this boy,' he said, 'it was not even a close shot, it was a kind of mid-shot. But I liked everything I saw about this guy – I liked the way he stood, I liked the way he talked and the way he impressed the lieutenant with the justice of their demand.'[30] It turned out to be Ayres – a 'hell of a find', according to Milestone – and, after being interviewed by Abbott, Milestone and the others, he was cast.[31] There was still Laemmle Junior to get through, and they took an instant dislike to each other (George Abbot also objected). Laemmle Junior didn't want Ayres, and tried to force a change of name on him to put him off, but Milestone was determined now and placed him in the cast. (Ayres and Junior later became friends, though he accused Junior of mismanaging his career after *All Quiet on the Western Front*). Though undoubtedly inexperienced, Ayres provided a superbly controlled performance of a sensitive young boy growing to manhood and rejecting the war he had entered with his enthusiastic classmates.

He went on to make a number of often disappointing films, before appearing in the classic comedy *Holiday* in 1938, and later as Dr Kildare in the long-running MGM series. His film career was interrupted by his conscientious objection to the Second World War – a brave, principled decision which provoked the wrath of many in Hollywood, led to accusations of cowardice, and saw his latest *Kildare* film pulled from some cinemas in the United States and Canada. MGM polled cinemas in twenty-one key cities to see whether they should continue to release Ayres' films. The result, no doubt to MGM's relief – they had over $1m invested in the pictures – was to release them.

14. Lew Ayres as Paul Bäumer – the image which made him a star
(author's collection)

Ayres' pacifism, which was not unknown at this time (he had told Louis B. Mayer, production head of MGM, in 1940 of his views), was linked only partly to his involvement with *All Quiet on the Western Front*. It had a subconscious influence, he admitted, but said that 'many things come together to create a man's outlook on life'.[32] Part of this was his deep immersion in philosophy, his religious interests and his vegetarianism, by which he illustrated his antipathy to murder of any kind. Ayres was a deep thinker, sensitive – a man quite unlike the traditional hedonist Hollywood dweller – who had held his views for many years. He said, when the controversy broke:

> It was in early childhood that I was first introduced to the Christian creed of nonresistance to evil. It is a vague and nebulous doctrine to the United States and it has taken years of gradual realization and patience for me to understand the full significance of its world-healing possibilities. ... Today I stand convinced that as like attracts like, hate generates hate, murder incites revenge, so charity and forgiveness reflect their kind, and the world's brotherhood will be made manifest not through economic experiences but through man's awakening to the irresistible power of love.[33]

Though Ayres was one of the boys, Milestone noticed that he was different from the others. 'I imagine the picture had a lot of influence on him,' he said, 'but he was always a very sensitive boy ... If the gang wanted to take a walk he used to stay in, if they wanted to stay in then he'd go out and walk by himself. He was a little different from everybody else, but he was a marvellous fellow, very sensitive.'[34]

Ayres was not one to shirk a responsibility, and served with great distinction in the medical corps. His career was blighted for a while, however. After the war he returned to Hollywood. He received an Academy Award nomination for his appearance in *Johnny Belinda* in 1948, and later went on to make films about the world's religions.

Remarque was very critical of Ayres, feeling that the Nazi menace precluded religious and moral scruples. However, he received some comfort from, unexpectedly, Hedda Hopper. On hearing that he had decided to be a conscientious objector, she wrote: 'I do not defend Lew, I merely defend his right to commit professional suicide if he wants to do it. Twelve years ago the world was acclaiming this same lad ... because he carried a great message against war in *All Quiet on the Western Front*. Now they stand ready to crucify him.'[35] Characteristically, Ayres was compassionate and tolerant towards those who had attacked him. 'I *knew* you couldn't go counter to what everyone else was feeling and not expect people to be resentful', he said. 'I didn't feel all those people treated me unfairly. That's ridiculous. I thought they'd be even more upset than they were.'[36]

It is possible to see something of Ayres in Paul Bäumer – indeed, the role could have been written for him. The film writer Herbert Luft said in 1978:

Ayres is a Renaissance man; he is science-oriented, interested in astronomy, mineralogy and meteorology. He plays the piano well, sometimes writing his own compositions. He and his wife are fond of art and antiques. He sketches and paints, having studied at art schools. He is also a writer. In many ways I imagine him as the man the young hero of *All Quiet on the Western Front* might have been if war had not destroyed him.[37]

There were noteworthy individuals playing other parts. Heinie Conklin, a Keystone Kop, played Hamacher, the patient with Bäumer and Kropp in the hospital. Fred Zinnemann – later to direct such classic films as *High Noon* (1952), *From Here to Eternity* (1953), *A Man for All Seasons* (1966) and *The Day of the Jackal* (1973) – played the parts of a German soldier and an ambulance-driver. Being an extra was not a fulfilling experience: after six weeks (he was paid $7.50 per day) he had had enough and, following a row with 'the rude first assistant, who was drunk with power', he was sacked.[38] It was the end of his acting career. Another who played a small part was Robert Parrish, the film editor and director. As a child actor he appeared in a number of films, including shooting his peashooter at Charlie Chaplin in *City Lights* (1931). In *All Quiet on the Western Front* he was one of the group of children who accuse Bäumer of cowardice when he returns to the classroom and tells them the truth about war.[39]

There were also some remarkable characters in the technical team. One was Otto Biber, a German army veteran, who taught the boys the goose-step. Milestone also employed Hans von Morhart and Hans Fuerberg, amongst others, as his advisers (it was rumoured that members of Carl Laemmle's large faemmle also worked on the picture). Von Morhart had served through the war with the German army; Fuerberg, in Potsdam when the war ended where he was serving as a cadet, was one of the few Germans to see the departure of the Kaiser from Germany. A critical role was played by the composer of the music: David Broekman, who in 1925 had composed the score for the silent classic *The Phantom of the Opera,* was hired. Finally, the work of Milestone's assistant, Nate Watt, should be recognised.

All Quiet on the Western Front gave George Cukor his first screen credit. A relative newcomer to the cinema at this time, Cukor was later to become famous for his direction of *What Price Hollywood?* (1932), *David Copperfield* (1935) and *The Philadelphia Story* (1940), among others. In October 1929 he was loaned to Universal to be dialogue director on *All Quiet.* He had come highly recommended: his agent was Myron Selznick, and he was friendly with Myron's brother, David, the brilliant producer (David Selznick was also a great friend of Lewis Milestone).

Cukor set to work getting the cast together. One of those he tested was Lew Ayres, though he was not impressed. Cukor's background was Broadway, where acting was more accomplished than in the early Hollywood sound period: according to Ayres, Cukor felt he was 'a nobody from nowhere. He was perfectly frank about saying I didn't have the polish.'[40]

Once the cast was in place, Cukor worked on dialogue. His approach – again, influenced by his Broadway experience – irritated the actors, who had to rehearse the same scenes time after time. Ayres called him the most prolific motivator he had known: 'Much of it was good, but there was too much to hang on to. Not just every scene, but every line of dialogue and every emphasis of the line. He had an incisive insight into his conception of the nature of the scene and of the personalities involved, and he was so articulate that he, to some extent, bound you to his thinking, to the degree that you couldn't really be free. You couldn't be yourself.'[41]

In contrast with the more relaxed Milestone, Cukor proved to be a burden – a burden present throughout the whole of filming. William Bakewell found him to be a perfectionist beyond belief: 'A plump fellow with black curly hair, horn-rimmed glasses and a scathing wit ... [Cukor] had a flair for caricaturing a bad dialogue reading so broadly, and with such waspish scorn, that the offender would never dare make that mistake again. His face would become almost gargoyle-like as he avidly mouthed each word along with us and urged us on in a dramatic scene.'[42]

Cukor's role was important, in some respects critical, in particular in his work with those young members of the team who were new to the cinema. Despite this, Milestone was reluctant to recognise his work and even, according to Cukor, argued against giving him the credit he deserved. Cukor said that he was not invited to the studio party at the end of production. He was surprised by all this as he regarded Milestone as a generous man and acknowledged that the strength and vitality of the film was due to him.[43]

That sour point came later. For now the team was together and the film was ready to enter production. There were still crucial details to finalise – the screenplay was to cause some problems during shooting – but the cast was ready. The next chapter sees how the cast, and others, took part in what was a difficult and costly production.

15. Lew Ayres experiencing the difficulties of life on the set
(author's collection)

4

The Troubled Production

All Quiet on the Western Front commenced production at eleven
o'clock on 11 November 1929, exactly eleven years after the
Armistice had been signed. This was a symbolic gesture by Carl
Laemmle, although his mind, no doubt, was on the publicity
value which could be generated (Harold Goodwin, who played
Detering, described it as a 'gag'[1]). The story was used extensively
in subsequent press material.

It was a difficult film to make. This was still the early sound
period, and technology was limited. What made things worse was
that this was a war picture: previous war films had mostly been
silent; this time, the sound of war had to be present along with
the sight of war. Samuel Hynes talks about the importance of
sound to *All Quiet on the Western Front* and *Westfront 1918* in his *A
War Imagined*, saying that 'Nothing like them had been, or could
have been done before':

> That they could be made in 1930 was partly a matter of film
> technology. Sound had been introduced, and soldiers in war
> films could now speak. More importantly, the noise of battle
> could be reproduced ... The volume of noise did more than
> add to the realism; it altered the balance in war films between
> men and the machinery of war. As a reviewer of *Hell's Angels*
> remarked: 'the noise of the propellers and machine guns

16. The crane used by Lewis Milestone to take the shots of the battle-field and training ground (BFI Stills, Posters and Designs)

keeps dialogue in its place.' It was another aspect of the Myth, in which the personal and the human were subordinated to the vast cacophonous machine.[2]

All Quiet on the Western Front had, for the first time in a war film, the sound of trench combat, what an enthusiastic recruit in the novel of *Paths of Glory* calls 'The Orchestration of the Western Front'.[3] The hissing of the bullets, the rattle of the machine-guns, the barrage, the howling and screaming of the injured and the frightened, were all too horribly apparent to the audience. It was so realistic, in fact, that, according to Milestone, on the opening night two veterans stood up when they saw some of the wounded and shouted that they were going to bring them back in.[4]

Another problem for Milestone was the camera. Whilst only a

few years earlier the cinema had got close to achieving the highest artistic standards – at the same time as providing entertainment for millions – the advent of talking pictures had interrupted progress. Cameras were noisy and microphones picked up the sound. By being placed in a sound-proof box, the camera went back to being a static instrument. Milestone, influenced strongly by the Russian masters, in particular Sergei Eisenstein – who, apparently, called *All Quiet on the Western Front* his graduation film – freed the camera, allowing fast and fluid shots of the trenches and No Man's Land. Helped by Edeson's 'barney', he created such a realistic view of war that scenes from the film resemble newsreel (and have sometimes been used as such).

Milestone also employed the huge crane which had been designed for use on the 1929 film *Broadway* (it had been developed by the director, Paul Fejos, and Hal Mohr, cinematographer). The crane enabled Edeson to get close-ups as the troops went over the top, even though explosions surrounded their advance.

Milestone wanted to re-create the experience of the soldier in the war. Considerable interest, therefore, was taken in the battlefield sets, the trenches and the German village. He was assisted by an experienced team. The sets were designed by William R. Schmitt and Captain Charles Hall, who had been an officer in the Canadian army (Hall, an Englishman, was Universal's regular art director, working on *Dracula*, *Frankenstein* and others). These two and Frank Booth (special effects cinematographer) were responsible for all the design, from the trenches to the German barracks. It was unquestionably a magnificent piece of work.

A whole village was built on the Universal backlot (this was not just for *All Quiet on the Western Front*; it was used for a number of later Universal productions). This remains today, where it is a staple part of the Universal Studio tour for holiday-makers attracted to the glamour of the movie studio. Although it is not the original set – this was destroyed in a fire in the late 1960s – it is still an impressive site. When I took the tour in 1991, I was impressed with how well it looked, although it was a bizarre experience as I was sharing my tram with a group of saffron-clad monks who devoted themselves to being embraced by the Wolf Man and having their photographs taken.

This was not the only location. The Irvine Ranch, sixty-six miles south of Hollywood, was used for the trench scenes, the forty-acre backlot at Pathé provided the river where the boys bathe and meet the French women, and Sherwood Forest in the San Fernando Valley was where the boys were filmed when they first go up the line. A *Universal Weekly* journalist who visited the Irvine Ranch in February 1930 provides an insight into the work which went into creating the set:

> The shell holes pock-marking No Man's land are real, made by blasts of dynamite, and are filled with muddy rain water. Near one of these is a rusting tomato can. ... Here are the German advance trenches, shallow and shell torn. For twenty-five yards in front of them is the barbed-wire work and on the barbs – caught there – are bits of cloth, of uniforms. They hang there to show where men have died. ... Back further are the line trenches, where the soldiers live. The walls are braced with branches of trees and saplings. Rainsoaked sandbags – a terrible slimy grey – offer protection.[5]

It was difficult to recreate the whole sickening mess of war (the censor would not allow that) – but Milestone got very close. Compare what he did, and what he was not able to do, with the description of an actual German trench by Roland Leighton, then the fiancé of Vera Brittain. He wrote from Loos in September 1915 (in an apparent rejection of her gift of a copy of Rupert Brooke's *1914*):

> [It] was captured by the French not so long ago and is pitted with shell-holes each big enough to bury a horse or two in. The dug-outs have been nearly all blown in, the wire entanglements are a wreck, and in among [this] chaos of twisted

17. Milestone's realistic portrayal of the battlefields of the war had the impact of contemporary newsreel (author's collection)

iron and splintered timber and shapeless earth are the fleshless, blackened bones of simple men who poured out their red, sweet wine of youth unknowing, for nothing more tangible than Honour or their Country's Glory or another's Lust of Power. Let him who thinks that War is a glorious golden thing, who loves to roll forth stirring words of exhortation, invoking Honour and Praise and Valour and Love of Country with as thoughtless and fervid a faith as inspired the priests of Baal to call on their own slumbering deity, let him look at a little pile of sodden grey rags that cover half a skull and a shin bone and what might have been Its ribs, or at this skeleton lying on its side, resting half-crouching as it fell, supported on one arm, perfect but that it is headless, and with the tattered clothing still draped around it; and let him realise how grand and glorious a thing it is to have distilled all Youth and Joy and Life into a foetid heap of hideous putrescence. Who is there who has known and seen who can say that Victory is worth the death of even one of these?[6]

The quest for authenticity was not just confined to the battle-field: the actors literally had to *be* soldiers. In addition to the drill by their German advisers, some of the boys had all their hair shaved to give the right military appearance. There was no room for fakes in the costume department, either. Universal purchased – for $27,500, they said – 250 genuine uniforms and field accessories which had been in use during the war. Each was a full kit: uniform, rifle and bayonet, gas-masks, spades, entrenching tools and cooking utensils. By a coincidence, the actors allocated the uniforms found that their stage name was actually in the uniform. *Universal Weekly* mentioned in passing that on some of the articles 'such as the gold braid of the epaulets on the officers' uniforms, the import duty ran as high as 90 percent of the cost.'[7]

The film set was so authentic that the chief sanitary inspector of Orange County made a visit to make sure that conditions were acceptable. He was accompanied by a nurse who had served at a US base hospital in Dijon for thirteen months during the war. On the set she met some of the veterans she had served with in France. The whole experience was a shock for her: 'It brings back to mind all the terrible anguish of that struggle,' she said.[8] It must have been bad: according to Arthur Edeson, the inspector shut the production down until it had been made safe. He said that, apart from the lack of real bullets, 'we might as well have been in the war'.[9]

Although a full screenplay had been completed by the time production started, adaptations needed to be made throughout. The screenplay, known as the Abbott version, had a similar structure to that which emerged finally in the film. There were some notable omissions from this version, however. The key omissions are as follows (some of these scenes were filmed – as surviving stills testify – but did not make the final cut).[10]

In the classroom where the boys imagine the glory of the war whilst Kantorek is lecturing:

- Kemmerich is being waved away from the railway station by his mother, who is dressed in black; Leer is rebuffed by a woman he is meeting in favour of a soldier in uniform (he is then seen walking down the street in uniform with a girl on each arm); Peter is seen leading a cavalry charge
- scene with Albert where he is debating whether he should enlist ('for', he writes, is that there will be no more classes and that he will see Paris; 'against' is that he might get shot and he will have to get up early)
- Müller takes Albert's paper and writes that it is bad that there will be no more school
- Behm imagines facing a bayonet charge terrified
- Paul imagines working at home on his writing, torn between his art and his duty

With Himmelstoss in the barracks and on the training ground:

- Paul and Albert forced to clean the floor with a toothbrush
- Himmelstoss practising and humiliating Behm and Bäumer in bayonet practice

On wiring duty:

- horses screaming when they are hit by shells
- longer attack sequence which lasts all night

In the billets after the death of Kemmerich:

- Paul reads letter from Kantorek giving them all his best wishes and calling them, once again, the Iron Men of Germany

Prior to visiting the French women:

- boys get Tjaden drunk, not Kat

Visiting the French women:

- each of the boys is seen, in turn, going into one of the bedrooms of the French women

(There is a significant change here. In the release version, Albert and Paul are injured. In the original script, all the surviving soldiers return to the front, where they talk about what they will do after the war.)

As Himmelstoss joins the assault:

- flame-throwers are used by the French to drive the German troops back

After the death of Duval:

- Paul is injured returning to his comrades; when he gets there he finds that Albert has also been injured and they are taken to hospital

In the hospital:

- lengthy scene where the nuns pray and the injured soldiers shout at them to be quiet

Back at home:

- Bäumer is upbraided by a major for not saluting

After Paul has left his father in the beer-garden:

- bumps into Müller – minus an arm – who is drunk
- conversation between Erna – Paul's sister – and Mrs Bäumer, where they talk about Paul not being happy
- Paul visits Mrs Kemmerich, where he assures her that her son died quickly and without pain

After Paul has berated Kantorek and left the classroom:

- Kantorek tells the class that Paul is suffering from shell-shock and calls upon them not to let him go back to the front alone; they all say enthusiastically that they will go

The ending proved to be a particular problem. Milestone knew that what he had filmed was not right and he wanted a different version. By now, however, the picture was complete and ready for release and Universal needed to recoup its investment. But Milestone still wanted to change the ending. In his book, Remarque had abandoned his first-person narrative in favour of a simple statement:

> He fell in October 1918, on a day that was so quiet and still on the whole front, that the army report confined itself to the single sentence: All quiet on the Western Front. ... He had fallen forward and lay on the earth as though sleeping. Turning him over one saw that he could not have suffered long; his face had an expression of calm, as though almost glad the end had come.[11]

This was difficult to translate into film. At least eight possible endings were suggested. The final version of the script suggested that the film finished with columns of men of all nations marching into a common grave. It went as follows:

> *Shot of the French sniper adjusting telescope sighter.* PAUL *has walked out into an open space, oblivious to his surroundings. He pauses. Across his face comes a vision of marching troops. They are German soldiers marching to 'Die Wacht am Rhine.' Another shadowy column comes from another angle, a column of French, marching to 'The Marseillaise.' Other columns march, and other anthems are merged into the music. The troops march toward a single point on the horizon and disappear into a common grave.* PAUL *is agitated in his dream. He calls out to stop the passing troops and finally leaps to his feet.*
>
> *Paul.* No, stop. No more! No more!
>
> *He stops abruptly and sinks down.*
>
> *Shot from above. As he rolls over, a trickle of blood runs down his forehead. There is a smile of peace and calm on his face.*[12]

The film then dissolves to the sound of a typewriter and the words 'All Quiet on the Western Front' double-exposed across Bäumer's face.

18. Bäumer found dead on the battlefield – one of the alternative
endings for the film (author's collection)

Milestone loathed this ending. He said that when he saw the
rushes he 'wanted to jump in after them.'[13] But he had nothing
to replace it with: 'I developed a blind spot and couldn't think of
anything,' he said. 'I labored under the delusion that we had to
stop the picture with a big crescendo finish. That was the blind
spot.'[14] Walking in the street one day, Karl Freund, the great
cinematographer, came into his mind. Freund had filmed magnificently the silent films, *The Last Laugh* (1924) and *Metropolis* (1926),
and Milestone believed that he was the man to make the ending
for *All Quiet on the Western Front*. However, he feared that he was
still in Germany and would not be able to help.

The next day Milestone bumped into Paul Kohner, the Hollywood producer, who told him that Freund had arrived in
Hollywood the day before. Milestone drove straight round to the
address Kohner left with him. Freund was having his dinner when

Milestone arrived, and he had to wait patiently for him to finish. He told him that he needed help with the end of the film and appealed to Freund as a German (a bad start – he was Czech!). When Freund saw the film he was excited enough to set to work. However, none of the endings they came up with was satisfactory.

The studio was now demanding that the film be finished (the theatre had been booked for the preview). Milestone asked for one more chance. They were booked into the Pathé lot in Culver City. 'While we were setting up the cameras it started to rain... I knew that I probably was washed up as well,' said Milestone.[15] Freund told him to send the company to the studio. As the two drove over, the solution was found. Milestone told Kevin Brownlow:

> it was raining cats and dogs ... and we had the windshield wiper going. And that was the rhythm. And I suddenly tuned in on what he was mumbling to himself. And what he was mumbling to the tempo of the windshield wiper, he was saying in German, der Schmetterling, der Schmetterling – which means butterfly ... So finally I said to him, what the hell are you mumbling about a butterfly? He said I don't know, but all I can tell you is that the finish must be as simple as a butterfly, [and] that's what started the whole thing.[16]

Back in the office Milestone consulted Remarque's book, which he had pinned up on the walls in sections. There he found that Bäumer was a butterfly collector and that he had given his collection to his sister. They had found their ending. As Bäumer sits in the trench near the end of the war he sees a butterfly just ahead. There is no fighting, and his comrades spend their time clearing the trench of water. A mouth-organ plays in the background. He tries to reach for the butterfly but fails. He then stands and his hand inches towards it. A French sniper shoots and kills him.

As both Edeson and Ayres had left by now, Freund had to operate the camera, and it was Milestone's hand in the final shot.

It was a great piece of cinematography (Freund's work so impressed Laemmle Junior that he gave him the directorial work on Universal's 1932 film *The Mummy*).

There was a further problem for Milestone. Carl Laemmle feared that the sombre nature of the film would put audiences off, and suggested that a happy ending be found. The request was abandoned when Milestone suggested that they have the Germans win the war![17]

As an experienced film editor, Milestone was able to cut the picture in his mind as he went along; indeed, he always spent considerable time prior to filming with storyboards (a practice which started with *All Quiet on the Western Front*). 'When I was filming,' he said, 'I knew exactly which sections of each scene would be shown, eventually, as long shots, medium shots, and close shots. So, as the scene went along, I stopped the camera directly the long-shot section was over, and moved to a medium or close shot, instead of shooting the entire scene right through from each position.'[18]

Milestone's genius was particularly evident in the editing of the first battle scene in the film. This involved many different shots, inside and outside the trench, and film overhead of the battlefield. Most of it was silent, except for the sound of bullets. He spent some time searching for the central theme of the battle. He told Kevin Brownlow:

> You know how [in] trench warfare, they used to send over wave after wave in the attack – came five o'clock in the morning, over the top, first wave then the second wave and the third and so on … I discovered the central idea for this … should be that when a machine gun shoots the man ought to drop with the same rapidity as the bullets leave the machine. And I thought if I keep that up, as wave after wave comes over, you have six, seven frames of the machine gun shooting and then immediately show the guys dropping, and they drop with the same impersonal, unemotional thing as

the machine gun spitting bullets … That became the central idea, and the rest is history.[19]

Some in the studio criticised Milestone's work on this scene. Seeing early rushes, they said that all that was on film was 'guys running from right to left and some … running from left to right'.[20] However, it was too early to judge. When one cut was completed, Milestone invited band leader Paul Whiteman (who was completing his own film, *King of Jazz*, at the studio) to view the copy. The fact that there was no sound failed to disappoint Whiteman, who told Milestone: 'If the rest of the picture is anything like this, you've got the winner of all time.'[21] Someone who had been intimately involved at the start, but had not seen a still or rushes, was Maxwell Anderson. When he did see the film, he was impressed: 'It is so real, it might have happened. It isn't a play or a film: it is real life,' he said.[22]

One unusual visitor to the studio was Albert Einstein (this may be an apocryphal story – Einstein was in Hollywood in late 1930 and did visit Universal, where he met Laemmle, but the timing is wrong for him to have viewed a pre-release copy as suggested here). Paul Kohner had invited the great scientist to visit Universal. Initially reluctant, Einstein agreed only on the basis that he would not be photographed (Carl Laemmle concurred, but did hide two cameramen behind trees). *All Quiet on the Western Front* had now been completed and Laemmle arranged for a viewing – 'obviously to convince the reluctant moviegoer that true works of art could emerge from Hollywood's film factories', according to Kohner's biographer. The cinema was packed with stars and directors who, though invited by Laemmle, had come to see Einstein. He was clearly moved by the film and then greatly surprised when Mary Pickford rushed up to him and kissed him on the hand. He had never heard of Mary Pickford.[23]

Many extras were needed for the film (150 were involved in the battle sequence). There was no help from the American army – Milestone said that they were not allowed to appear in a foreign uniform – so help was sought from the Santa Ana and Hollywood posts of the American Legion. Universal claimed that 2,000 veterans responded to their request for extras for the film (only First World War soldiers were wanted, but some who had fought in the Spanish war also volunteered). As German, French, English, American, Italian, Canadian, Australian and Russian veterans converged on the studio, *Universal Weekly* proudly said that 'War hatreds and international enmities [were] forgotten and swept aside, as they were in … Remarque's masterpiece, [as] these two thousand, many of whom had fought on opposite sides, assembled enthusiastically for the greatest war picture for peace ever conceived.'[24]

It was not an easy life. Fred Zinnemann talked about the life of an extra on the film. He said that they were taken to the various sets 'by bus in the pre-dawn December darkness'. He continued: 'The shooting day started at 9.00 a.m.; we did not get back to Hollywood until 8.00 p.m. – sometimes later. The production people kept us working hard and got their money's worth. Marching through deep mud in heavy artificial rain and wearing wet clothes all day was not necessarily a lot of fun; but sometimes there were days when we lounged on hospital cots, being bandaged.'[25]

It was inevitable, in making such a film, that there would be casualties and injuries. There was one fatality when an extra fell against a building in Universal City in the French village set. Milestone also said that there was an unpleasant experience with a veteran who suffered from shell-shock. The company had agreed that no one with shell-shock would be employed. However, a sufferer had got through and was an extra in one of the battle scenes. He was sent away. Milestone himself was injured, though this was minor: his tin hat saved him from a more serious injury.

That there were no injuries on the battlefield shots was down to Milestone's explosives man, Harry Lonsdale. Lonsdale exploded each shell with the virtuosity of an orchestral conductor using a switchboard control. He knew where all the dynamite had been

19. The troops enjoy chocolate on the set. Milestone and Cukor can be seen at the back (BFI Stills, Posters and Designs)

buried, which proved to be useful when one extra fell on twenty pounds of explosive.

Although it was a tough film to make there was plenty of joking on the set. As befits a comic, much of this came from Slim Summerville, who would flick bits of paper at the other actors (he did this so hard that they stung) and hide used chewing gum behind their ears. Milestone joined in all this. One day, some of the boys heard that Ernst Lubitsch had said that with all the adulation and news coverage for the film he hoped that this would not make Milestone big-headed. Subsequently, all the cast and crew formed an aisle, down which (and *over* his prostrate assistant, Nate Watt) a Teutonic-looking Milestone strode. This was photographed and sent to Lubitsch. The message said: 'Director Lewis Milestone arrives on the set for a day's work.'[26]

All the problems associated with the shoot meant that *All Quiet on the Western Front* went well over budget. Although the scenes shot and footage exposed were almost on target (at 459 scenes, only an additional 4 had been shot and there was a positive balance of 2,899 feet of footage), the shooting days more than doubled. Originally, it was estimated that 48 days would be needed; by the end of production 99 days had been used. This, together with other cost overruns, particularly on salaries, but also on properties, sets and other direct costs, led to the budget growing from $891,000 to over $1.4m (see table opposite). This was a disaster for the Laemmles, and for their poverty-stricken studio. Studio executives must have thought their worst fears had come true.

Once *All Quiet on the Western Front* had been completed, Universal prepared a silent version for their own theatres (the company was one of the last exhibitors to convert to sound) and for overseas release, again for those cinemas not yet wired. The silent version was shown in France and Australia, and possibly elsewhere, though never in Britain.

Surviving actors from the film deny that a silent version ever existed. It does exist, however (it is possible that none of those involved ever saw the film). The Library of Congress holds three versions: the first is about 88 minutes in length; the other two are both 133 minutes, with one having synchronised sound (the orchestration provided by David Broekman, who did the music for the sound version). Broekman's sound effects were mainly martial tunes, cheering and singing, sounds of boots marching, explosions and bullets, and orchestral music. The intertitles were written by Walter Anthony, Universal's chief title-writer.

The silent version is similar to the sound: most of the shots are the same, although (in the longest print) there is no beer-garden sequence, and the scene with the French women is reduced. There are some nice additions. At one point Bäumer and Himmelstoss are seen jousting with long sticks; there is a

Account	Estimate	Final cost
Salaries		
Stock talent	1,500.00	2,700.00
Picture talent	77,000.00	162,859.23
Extra talent	70,000.00	100,930.79
Director	40,050.00	67,591.67
Director's staff	30,000.00	64,387.13
Story	25,000.00	25,197.19
Continuity	34,080.00	34,079.15
Raw film	21,800.00	26,735.59
Lab charges	12,720.00	16,303.28
Set operation	5,000.00	11,997.94
Sound effects	12,650.00	17,361.02
Wardrobe	17,500.00	46,959.15
Properties	35,500.00	63,455.77
Sets/miniatures	154,250.00	222,902.38
Transportation	12,500.00	38,832.04
Location and maintenance	35,000.00	65,917.31
Titles/dialogue	15,000.00	19,501.84
Film editing	3,450.00	13,412.93
Lighting, labour, current	33,000.00	67, 015.97
Ranch and zoo charges	5,000.00	6,740.49
Special rolling stock	2,500.00	534.58
Miscellaneous	5,500.00	24,151.01
Studio charge 12.5%	92,812.00	0
TOTAL DIRECT COST	741,812.00	1,099,566.46
Retained time	50,000.00	50,085.00
Scenario department overhead	25,000.00	25,750.00
General overhead 7.5%	55,688.00	241,472.43
Sound overhead	18,500.00	31,989.50
GRAND TOTAL	891,000.00	1,448,863.39

Note: there is an error in the original calculation, which was five cents out. This has been corrected.

low shot of Himmelstoss marching in step when the boys are diving in the mud; when Bäumer and Albert are injured they are seen covered in sheets comforting one another, and, near the end, there is a beautiful overhead shot of the sky just after the intertitle reads 'A quiet day on the Western Front'.

There are few opportunities to see how a silent film was developed from a sound version. Of particular interest are the intertitles. Most of these correspond to actual dialogue in the film. The scene where Paul Bäumer returns to the classroom is a good example:

> Kantorek: Bravely they went to the front – bravely they fought and died – now they call to you, the Iron Youth of Germany!
> [Bäumer enters and Kantorek shakes his hand]
> Kantorek: This is Paul Bäumer, who heard his country's call though my poor lips.
> Kantorek: Look at him, bronzed and sturdy – the kind of soldier *you* should be!
> [Boys look at Bäumer admiringly]
> Kantorek: Tell them some of the glorious things you've seen and done, Paul.
> Bäumer: I can't tell them anything.
> Kantorek: Can't you tell them how their country needs them at the front.
> [Bäumer looks angry]
> Kantorek: Then tell some deed of heroism you have done.
> Bäumer: We live with the rats – we burrow like rabbits – and we try not to be killed – but most of us are.
> [Boys look confused]
> Bäumer: I'm sick of lies – death is hideous – there's no glory in the mud!
> Kantorek: That's not what we speak of here, Paul.
> Bäumer: Of course it isn't! You tell them of banners – and glory – and the martial music of bands – but we who fight and die know better.

Bäumer: You want me to tell them how they're needed out
there.

[Bäumer faces boys]

Bäumer: He tells you that it's sweet to die in battle – but he
knows nothing about it.

[Boys jump up, gesticulate angrily. Bäumer turns to Kantorek]

Bäumer: I'm sorry, but it's *not* sweet to die in battle – it's
hideous!

Bäumer: There's only one thing worse than dying out there
– and that's living out there.

[Bäumer leaves classroom]

Though similar to the sound film, the silent version does stand
up well as a film in its own right. Contrary to the legend, ZaSu
Pitts was replaced in this version as well.

All Quiet on the Western Front was a difficult production. It was
hard work, often uncomfortable, dirty and wet, and the days
were always long. The uneasy transition to sound meant that
Milestone and his team were pioneers. Having got to the end,
they were confident that they had made a great film. But the
substantial budget overrun showed that this would need a big
box office to justify the investment and give Universal their return.
The studio executives must have anticipated with some nervousness, and with considerable uncertainty, how their film would be
judged. Chapter 5 shows how right they were to be nervous,
although the problems they faced were not immediate ones.

5

Reception, Condemnation
and Censorship

All Quiet on the Western Front as film was received in the same
way as *All Quiet on the Western Front* as book: massive audiences, enthusiastic critics, great controversy. In no country, and
by no censor's office, did the film remain untouched. For most
there were small cuts made, but they were not minor changes:
any deletions were serious as they removed the realism of Milestone's work. In some countries the film was cut more heavily,
and then banned. In Germany and Austria it provided the focus
for political turmoil, with violent demonstrations and government
intervention. Few films before – or, indeed, since – have been
attacked, censored and condemned in this way. Within a few
short months a classic had been ripped apart; by the time the
film had run its initial course, there was no longer a full print
available, and one would not exist for fifty-four years. Even then
this was a German reconstruction; work on a complete English
language version started only in 1997.

Those involved with the film would have been delighted, though
not surprised, at the acclaim it got. The reception had fulfilled
Universal's publicity, which had promised a:

20. An advertisement for the film in New Zealand in 1930
(The New Zealand Film Archive)

*Remarque*able Story
*Remarque*able Cast
*Remarque*able Director
*Remarque*able Picture

The *American Cinematographer* had led the way: 'Universal has a picture that should go down as one of the greatest war pictures ever filmed,' it said in March 1930.[1] *Variety* called it a 'harrowing, gruesome, morbid tale of war, so compelling in its realism, bigness and repulsiveness. ... Nothing passed up for the niceties; nothing glossed over for the women. Here exhibited is war as it is, butchery.' It recommended that the League of Nations should distribute it in every language to be shown every year 'until the word War shall have been taken out of the dictionaries'.[2]

Louella Parsons in the *Los Angeles Examiner* was also impressed. 'Ambitious emperors and greedy war lords would not be so eager to encourage men to kill each other if they could be induced to look at *All Quiet on the Western Front*,' she said, 'No book, no play and certainly no motion picture could possibly be more effective in preaching the doctrine of peace than this amazing story by Erich Maria Remarque.' She went on:

> Universal has made a very remarkable picture ... which tells the story of the war from the German angle. Very deftly, very delicately, with infinite good taste, Lewis Milestone has directed this difficult story. There is no favoritism shown Germany, and no attempt made to discriminate between countries. The blame for the slaughter of innocent boys is laid at the door of all those who were responsible for the war.[3]

The *Los Angeles Evening Herald* said that it was better than *Journey's End*: '[that told] of an officer's war, while *All Quiet* is a private's war and on the losing side. Here hunger and the foreknowledge of defeat are as deadly foes as the enemy in the trenches a few hundred yards away.'[4] In its première week, excellent business was done with an outstanding $22,000 taken at the Carthay Circle.

In New York the film ran at the Central Theater for twenty-three weeks with five shows daily. It then moved to the Roxy, which was known as the Cathedral of Film with its 6,200 seats. Ginger Rogers, then a rising film star, was invited to the première. In her autobiography, published sixty-one years later, she recalled the experience:

> Movie premières were lavish and dazzling events in those days. Everyone who was anyone came dressed to the nines. Mother and I put on our long evening gowns and joined the excited throng that gathered in the tiny foyer of the Central Theater. The V.I.P.s from the business world were joined by the Hollywood stars who happened to be in Manhattan. We brushed shoulders with Vilma Banky, Ben Lyon, and Rod La Rocque and saw Bebe Daniels, Douglas Fairbanks, Sr., and Lilyan Tashman. Reporters and photographers were

everywhere. The cameraman's powder flashes went off like lightning in a bottle, making the foyer look like a shower of meteors inside a tinsel box. Though it was April, ladies wore gorgeous long evening coats and capes trimmed with silver and white fox, ermine, mink, and sable. Diamonds sparkled on throats and around wrists. Gentlemen were attired in black tie or white tie and tails and sported black derbies or top hats. Evening clothes were special in those days and dressing up was the norm.[5]

She fell in love with Lew Ayres that night and they were later to marry (and subsequently divorce).

The 'applause at the end of the première was thunderous', according to Ginger.[6] It was matched by the reviews. The *New York Times* said it gripped the audience in almost total silence and claimed that some of the battle scenes resembled actual newsreel – a great tribute to Milestone, who was the first to admit that he had never seen a battlefield (the newspaper later voted the film as one of the ten best of the year).[7] This was also recognised by Howard Barnes in the *Herald Tribune*:

> In … [Milestone's] hands the screen rediscovers many of the qualities that distinguished it while speechless, and were so wantonly discarded with the advent of sound. He has thought always in terms of the camera, and his sound accompaniment is never allowed to break the episodic movement of the show. His war scenes are certainly the most vivid and effective ever brought to the screen.[8]

Finally, *The Nation* called the film 'a terrifying document that reveals the carnage of war with staggering force … [and which] surpasses [all previous battle scenes on film] in the stark horror and madness of the business of fighting.' It preferred *Journey's End* as drama, though.[9]

Photoplay carried a dull review, although it later awarded *All Quiet on the Western Front* its gold medal as best film of the year.

'The efforts to screen ... [Remarque's] powerful portrayal of the effects of war', it said, 'is a huge undertaking and almost certain to fall short of perfection. Not a real master-picture, but it does give a realistic story of the war experiences that happen to any youth. The daily intimate experiences are impressive, the battle scenes tremendously dramatic.'[10] A more critical review was in the left-wing *New Masses* by the radical writer Harry Alan Potamkin. He said:

> A war film cannot be evaluated simply as entertainment or an isolated production; it must be criticized for what it implies and what it omits. ... The failure of *All Quiet on the Western Front* is that of the treatment. The film lacks the structure it deserves, the heroic structure. In none of these films of the continent or America has war been actually and inferentially presented for what it is: the peak of a competitive society.[11]

Another was in the New York *Evening Post*. Thornton Delehunty said:

> All these things have been doggedly incorporated – the screaming shells, the stabbing bayonets, the waste of life and youth, the ribaldries behind the front lines – and yet they emerge on the screen as lifeless copies, pale shadows which fail to catch, except in only occasional moments, the vitality and emotional sincerity which leapt out from the pages of the book. ... It is impossible to view the picture without sensing this overanxiety to hit the nail on the head.[12]

Marlene Dietrich, who was to become romantically involved with Remarque later, saw the film in Hollywood. She wrote to her husband, 'It's a tremendous success here. Fascinating that it's the same Remarque I used to see at Mutzbauer's. Please send me the book. I want to read it in German the way he wrote it.'[13] And Howard Hughes told Milestone that he thought the picture would be better than the book (though he had not read it). He liked particularly the shell-hole sequence and the school-house scene where Bäumer comes back and tells the boys about the reality of war. Hughes congratulated Milestone on forcing such a remarkable performance out of Ayres; he had seen *The Kiss* and had not rated him.[14]

There were some problems with state censor offices, despite the fact that Universal had liaised openly with the Motion Picture Producers and Distributors of America (MPPDA – known colloquially as the Hays Office after its first president, Will Hays) throughout.[15] Even trailers had to be approved, and they had to check that there was no copyright outstanding on the title, as the Mills Corporation had released a song previously with the same name. Universal must have thought that they had got it right from the start. Colonel Jason Joy of the MPPDA – reporting on a meeting with Del Anderson (*sic*) – told the company that the subject matter demanded a literal interpretation of the novel:

> I am inclined to believe that its truth and simplicity, its subtle preachment against war, and its equally subtle pleading for an appreciation of the 'abnormalities' of those who participate in the war, will carry such a tremendous appeal as to make it possible for you to treat the various episodes which occur in the book with a boldness and truthfulness which I think you would be unwise to employ in a story of less merit.[16]

Though MPPDA officers warned Universal about certain scenes – those containing anti-French and anti-English comments, the severed hands, nudity and a few others – they praised the company for the screenplay which resulted. Such warnings were repeated after the première, but the MPPDA was clearly impressed. Their officer at the event reported that this was 'A very faithful adaptation ... The spirit of the book has been exceedingly well portrayed. Direction is splendid and the acting uniformly excellent. The entire picture is devoted to showing the gruesomeness, horror and futility of war. In detail and in theme it is thoroughly gruesome.' He then provided a unique picture of the atmosphere:

> On the whole the picture held the audience very well. There were times (at the very first) when there was a considerable buzzing of conversation to be heard. Later the audience became thoroughly engrossed in the picture and at times were so quiet that one could have heard a pin drop. There was no applause at the end of the film but the line spoken by Kat when he says that at the next war all the statesmen should be put in a field and given clubs so that they can fight it out among themselves received a great deal.[17]

In Ohio, the scenes of the naked men swimming and parts of the fraternisation scene with the French women were deleted (this was cut also in New York and Pennsylvania, in Massachusetts in the 1934 reissue, although in this case the cuts were required for Sunday showings only). These scenes survived in Kansas, but, for some reason, part of the sequence of Himmelstoss being beaten by the boys was cut. Some profanities and suggestive dialogue were also removed in Pennsylvania.

More seriously, the film attracted the attention of Major Frank Pease, manager of the Hollywood United Technical Directors Association (UTDA), a right-wing pressure group of uncertain size. Pease pursued a dual campaign, which aimed to stop the national release of *All Quiet on the Western Front* and persuade Paramount to kick Sergei Eisenstein, a 'Bolshevik murderer and robber',[18] he believed, out of the country, as both represented pacifism. (Eisenstein had been brought to Hollywood by Jesse Lasky in 1930 to 'inject a dash of freshness and vigour into ... American film', according to Marie Seton, one of his biographers.)[19]

Pease was a well-known American Fascist, later to be commander of the International Legion Against Communism, and later still to be 'unmasked as a German agent, the unsuccessful organizer of Fascist detachments in the shadow of the Statue of

Liberty', according to Eisenstein.[20] In collaboration with others, including the notorious Representative Hamilton Fish, he kicked up such a fuss that eventually Eisenstein left the United States for Mexico. He was not so successful with *All Quiet on the Western Front*, however, although his vindictive campaign led to some nervousness in Hollywood, even if throughout he could not spell correctly the title of the film.

Pease really did not like this film. According to the UTDA Report, *All Quiet on the Western Front* was rated bad – the lowest category – for story, scenario, direction, technical direction; for plausibilities of plot, situations, characterisations, backgrounds, dramatic logic; for military etiquette; for military ceremonials; interpretation of death; treatment of blasphemy, the Ten Commandments, marriage, civilised conventions of sex and the double-entendre; and for *lèse-majesté* of nations, institutions and individuals.

Sadly, his remarks have not survived (these were usually written on the back of the form), but his views have. In a telegram sent to President Hoover, government officers, military offices of foreign governments, and editors, amongst many others, Pease said:

> May we solicit your great influence to help prohibit further showing without drastic censoring and revision of Universal's film *All's Quiet on the Western Front* [*sic*]? This is the most brazen propaganda film ever produced in America. It undermines beliefs in the army and in authority. Moscow itself could not have produced a more subversive film. Its continued uncensored exhibition especially before juveniles will go far to raise a race of yellow streaks slackers and disloyalists. Domestic statecraft common sense and plain every day patriotism demand instant suppression of such vicious propaganda. It is important to act promptly. Accept please our every respect and thanks.[21]

Copying the telegram to Franklin Roosevelt, governor of New York State, on 28 April 1930, he added:

> My dear Sir, I recommend this vile film to everyone's hostility and scorn. Its evil aim is straight against the military establishments of the whole civilized world. *It transcends all national boundaries* in the power of its corrupt appeal, and this is a defensive concern of all responsible classes and institutions everywhere. If such a malicious film is allowed to proceed unchecked, *and to make money*, we can depend on it that the lawless, ignorant, unrestrained and imitative cinema producers here will simply flood our country (and the world) with even worse films, the moment they discover such scurvy 'realism' and extreme propaganda *pays*. The Mesopotamium mongrels guilty of such criminal films were bound some time to over-reach themselves, and this looks like the time. It is the boldest attempt at international corruption yet made in the American Cinema. May we hope that you will not let this filthy film pass without your severest scrutiny and your strongest repudiation. I hope there is still guts enough left in America to crush vipers. With all thanks for your honored help, I am
>
> Sincerely yours,
> Major Frank Pease, Pres.[22]

Universal – who had been alerted to the attack by Colonel Wingate of the MPPDA – was sufficiently concerned that it hired an agency to investigate Pease and offered to show the film to Roosevelt, Hoover and others in government. R. H. Cochrane, vice-president of the company, replied to Wingate:

> Frankly, the man seems mad and frothing at the mouth. He manifests the same Prussian spirit which, without doubt, brought on the world war – the spirit which made war something to be idolized. When war is glorified and painted as the highest desideratum, I imagine Major Pease is well pleased, but apparently he cannot stand the stark truth. ...

The world-wide popularity of Mr. Remarque's book was not an accident. It told a story that the world accepted with keenest interest. It was bitterly assailed, but the attacks always came from men who never want the truth to be told about war.[23]

One organisation Pease had sent his letter to – The Boy Scouts of America – responded vigorously to the MPPDA, providing one of the best reviews of the film. They felt that there was nothing to justify Pease's accusations: 'Everything depicted and said actually takes place in any war,' they said. They continued:

The same basic emotions are ever present when Nations fly at each other's throats. Some of the scenes are horrible, some base and sordid, but that is war. ... If all legislators, all voters, all 'makers of wars' in all countries were forced to view this picture, or others like it, occasionally, Nations would be less anxious to make war upon one another. ... The picture is bitter medicine, but good for what ails nations. I hope it runs for a long time.[24]

They were joined by *The Nation*, which commented: '*Aux armes, citoyens!* The foundations of society are threatened again, but the gods be praised, the Hollywood Technical Directors' Institute stands between us and destruction.' They concluded: 'When Major Pease sees thousands of people crowding to see [*All Quiet on the Western Front*], what must he think of human nature?'[25]

Apart from Pease and his cronies, the reception was positive – and often magnificent. *All Quiet on the Western Front* gathered an array of awards. In the Academy Awards for 1929–30, the first voted on by Academy members and not by the handful of judges who had made decisions previously, the film was nominated for best picture, direction, writing and cinematography (none of the actors was successful). Arthur Edeson lost out to Joseph T. Rucker and Willard Van Der Veer for *With Byrd at the South Pole*, and Abbott, Anderson and Andrews to Frances Marion for *The Big*

House. *All Quiet on the Western Front* did, however, take the top awards of best picture (against *The Big House*, *Disraeli*, *The Divorcee* and *The Love Parade*) and best direction, with Milestone beating Clarence Brown (*Anna Christie*), Robert Leonard (*The Divorcee*), Ernst Lubitsch (*The Love Parade*) and King Vidor (*Hallelujah*). Louis B. Mayer presented Carl Laemmle with the award.

Ironically, given that the original review was lukewarm, the film was awarded the *Photoplay Magazine* gold medal for best picture of 1930: 'the highest distinction that can be earned by a motion picture', 'the Nobel prize of filmdom', according to the magazine.[26] The medal – 123.5 pennyweights, two-and-a-half inches in diameter and solid gold (designed and executed by Tiffany and Company, New York) – was presented to Universal Pictures. As this was the award of readers, it showed the extent to which the film had captured the imagination of cinemagoers. Previous winners of the gold medal included *The Big Parade* (1925), *Seventh Heaven* (1927) and *Four Sons* (1928), all of which had a war theme.

All the awards were deserved and justified. There was an unexpected downside, however. They were listed at the beginning of the film on reissue, replacing the poetic foreword which had opened the original release. Given the importance of this statement to the film (and to the book) this was a pointless, and somewhat tragic, omission.

The film was released in Canada in June 1930 in a censored version. The deletions were as follows:[27]

- dialogue in reel 3 'When you come back you'll all get some nice clean underwear'
- close-up of boy in hysterics in reel 4
- dialogue as soldiers are discussing what to do after the war in reel 8:
  Leer: 'Get drunk and look for women'
  Tjaden: 'and when I find her, nobody would see me for two weeks'

- eliminate words 'in the backside' from line spoken by Kat 'I ought to give you a kick in the backside'
- eliminate Paul stabbing French soldier and holding his mouth; eliminate close-up of staring face of dead man; eliminate close-up of French soldier's face
- delete one-minute incident with French women

Ironically, in Britain (where film censorship was strong, and censors had cut some war films heavily), *All Quiet on the Western Front* fared better than in other countries. There was only one small cut – 201 feet deleted from the bedroom scene. In a cable to the New Zealand censor, the British Board of Film Censors (BBFC) said that they consider it a 'wonderfully realistic representation [of] war with minimum national bias. After censorship excellent weekly press comments.'[28] It should be noted that more may have been cut – there is no record of British censorship for this period, as documentation was destroyed in the Second World War. Certainly, British censors were keen to remove much of what they felt was controversial material from films of the period, and those which dealt with war and peace issues were often targeted heavily.

The film opened successfully in the Alhambra and Royal Cinemas in the West End (the first to open with simultaneous first runs). Lloyd George, who knew more than most about military incompetence and brutality, called it 'a perfectly marvellous film ... the most outstanding war film I have ever seen'.[29] Reviewers were just as impressed. Sydney Carroll in the *Sunday Times* was clearly shocked by the realism of Milestone's work. 'I hate it,' he said. He continued:

> It made me shudder with horror. It brought the war back to me as nothing has ever done before since 1918. ... No detail of horror has been spared to us. The dangers, the savageries, the madness of war, and the appalling waste and destruction of youth, the shattering of hopes, illusions, beliefs, the futility

of patriotism and nationalism – all these are depicted with relentless veracity, unshrinking crudity, and on a scale as colossal as the world-war itself.[30]

For James Agate it was one of the best films ever made, even though he was not moved and would have preferred it as a silent rather than sound film: 'I suppose I expected to receive at least the impression of what must be the most sickening thing in war – its dreadful stench,' he wrote. 'There is a passage in some other war book in which a soldier describes his horror when first he felt the ground give beneath his feet, and discovered that he was treading not upon earth but upon a dead man. There is nothing of this in the present film.'[31]

A more enthusiastic review came from 'Looker On' in the left-wing *Reynolds News*, who called it a wonderful picture: 'It is the protest of youth against its exploitation by older men, who, under the illusion that fighting is a glorious and necessary thing, throw the boys into the hell of war – turn them into cannon fodder. All the fighting, attack, counter-attack, bombardment, is tragically real, and the fear which is contained in these young men is not only understandable but inevitable. And when there is no fighting it is nearly all mud and filth, brutality and misery.'[32]

The reviewer praised Lew Ayres, and Louis Wolheim in particular, whose performance surpassed all his other work. Wolheim also came in for praise from the reviewer in *The Times*, though he seems to have missed the point of the ending: 'It is the supreme merit of the film', he said 'that it contrives to suggest in its final scenes the soldiers' lack of enthusiasm, their recognition of defeat and their willingness to go on fighting to the last.'[33]

The trade journals were also impressed. *Kinematograph Weekly* said that as an 'indictment of the futility of war it is as great as the book was; no praise could be higher than that'.[34] *Bioscope* said it was a 'Remarkable film adaptation of a world-renowned book':

A powerful indictment of modern warfare which, while conveying a strong moral lesson, is of extraordinary entertainment value. Its skilful characterisation, emotional appeal, with relief of humour and dramatic realism, make it of engrossing interest throughout its length. The greatest war picture yet produced. ... Every picture theatre is morally bound to show it.[35]

The film was also acclaimed by some of the more heavyweight writers and critics. C. A. Lejeune, despite having difficulty with parts of the film, said that it showed 'without compromise, and in its own medium, the complete futility and waste and bestiality of war'.[36] In his book *Celluloid*, published a year after the release of the film, Paul Rotha praised the film's realism. Universal, he said, had made a remarkable film, one, moreover, whose pacifism had gone further than Remarque's work; he claimed it was 'destined to go down to posterity as a true and faithful record of the War'. According to Rotha, Universal had recognised this and had donated copies of the film to corporations and councils in England to act as a permanent record of the conflict. Whether this actually happened is open to question: no city councils contacted could trace a copy, or provide any supporting material, although it is of interest to note that the copy held by the National Film Archive, which is one of the most complete, was donated by the Corporation of Manchester.

Rotha disliked parts of Ayres' performance and the choice of Beryl Mercer for the mother, and did not rate Milestone as highly as others had done (he later revised his opinion after seeing *The Front Page*). Even with all this, he concluded, 'whatever we may say of it, *All Quiet on the Western Front* has been acknowledged the handiwork of genius and the masterpiece of the century. Who are we to deny that?'[37]

The first country to ban *All Quiet on the Western Front* was New Zealand on 20 June 1930, and the film was released only following cuts and an appeal. Mr W. A. Tanner, the then chief censor of films, said that it was banned because it was not entertainment. In one of the most spectacular misjudgements of a film ever made, he said it was 'Suggestive in parts. Packed with the nauseating side of war from start to finish. Its only merit is that it is claimed to be an indictment of war and strong peace propaganda. This is doubtful.' He concluded: 'In any case it is a question whether the screen should be used for propaganda of any kind.'[38]

Universal set to work to overturn the decision. They sent a cable to the British Board of Film Censors asking them why they had passed the film. The reply was sent to the New Zealand Censor's Office, leading Mr Tanner to believe that the company was engaged in underhand work. He passed the reply to the under-secretary with a note. It seems he really did not wish to see the film released: 'I do not consider the film version of "All Quiet" a suitable picture for exhibition in New Zealand,' he said. 'In my view it is not in the public interest. This view has been upheld by an independent Board of Appeal constituted under the New Zealand law.'[39]

It was out of Tanner's hands, however, by now. The Crown Law Office advised the under-secretary that, for Universal, 'The only course open appears to be to make such alterations in the film as will render it substantially a different production from that which was originally submitted and then to submit it over again to the Censor for examination as a different film.'[40] A number of deletions were made. These were:

- cuts eliminating the word 'guts' in two passages of dialogue in reel four and the passage 'When we come back I'll get you all some nice clean underwear'
- cut eliminating the phrase 'and look for women' from the passage of dialogue 'Get drunk – and look for women' in reel nine
- cuts of scenes to tone down the sequence of Paul Bäumer in the shell-hole with the dying Frenchman
- cuts eliminating objectionable shots of men bathing in river, opening parts of sequence when men prepare to cross river at night to get to the girls and the elimination of the entire

section when the three men visit the girls and spend the night
with them

The Board of Appeal passed the film eventually, though for 'Adult
Audiences only', but this was not unanimous. The under-secretary
wrote to Tanner that the chairman 'felt that your rejection of the
film in the first instance was justified, as it not only enabled a
second opinion to be taken, but also it afforded fuller opportunity for its consideration and reconstruction [sic].'[41]

Such censorship problems seemed to have been overcome by
the time the film received its première at the Civic in the presence
of the governor-general. When it was later shown publicly, no
interval was offered. An advertisement stated, 'In order that the
atmosphere of realism shall not be disturbed there will be NO
INTERVALS during the performance.'[42]

The film was again banned just after the outbreak of the
Second World War, when nine films were withdrawn because of
their anti-war tone. Joseph Breen of the MPPDA warned omin-
ously that, 'during the duration of the war, films containing anti-
war propaganda or a strong expression of pacifist sentiment will
not be approved by the New Zealand censor, or, alternatively,
will be subject to excisions.' Surviving records do not indicate
which were the other eight films.[43]

All Quiet on the Western Front did not suffer as much political
controversy in Australia, though there were more deletions. Both
sound and silent versions were submitted to the censor; the sound
was viewed in June 1930 and the silent six months later. The
deletions were as follows:[44]

- close-ups of recruits' faces as they rise from the mud drill
- dialogue 'Last night … this is the first time I have been able
  to get the wrinkles out of my guts'; word 'guts' used by
  Wolheim on wagon; Wolheim saying to recruit 'Never mind –
  it's happened to better men than you and me. When we get
  back I'll get you some nice clean underwear'

- Wolheim twice hitting boy on jaw, and word 'guts' from dialogue in reel five
- in first attack scene, considerable reductions to machine gun fire, and men being mown down before barbed wire; reductions to scenes of hand-to-hand fighting in trenches, in particular to close-up shots of men being bayoneted and struck down with clubbed rifles
- in the discussion between men on what they will do after the war, first reference to women and man holding up gun ring and saying 'When I meet the Cinderella this garter fits you will not see me for a fortnight'; Wolheim saying 'Who started this ... I'll kick your backside'
- considerable reductions to bombardment of churchyard
- close-up of boy stabbing French soldier and subsequent shots up to where the star shell bursts; close-up of Frenchman's face in light of star shell
- reductions to scene where men upend themselves in the river as the French women walk by; soldiers exposing themselves as they undress
- deletions to scene where gramophone is running, and all subsequent scenes to point where troops are marching (this includes part of the scene where the boys spend the night with the French women)

Seven minutes were cut in total – including some of the most important parts of the film – and it was classified as not being suitable for children. The silent version suffered similar cuts, and a number of subtitles were deleted corresponding to the cuts in dialogue in the sound version. This did not prevent critical acclaim, however. The *Sydney Morning Herald* called it a 'magnificent production'. *The Daily Pictorial* said this 'superbly directed film must be classed as one of the most brilliant achievements of the screen. ... All previous war films fade into insignificance when compared with this screen classic.'[45]

In Denmark the film was released in a cut edition and in English in August 1930 (it was not until 1950 that the Danes had the opportunity to see the original version). Generally reviewers found it gripping, said it had been filmed with imagination and excellent technical skill and praised the decision to use unknown actors for some of the lead roles.

Though difficult for Universal, the troubles in New Zealand and Australia (and more modest cuts elsewhere) were nothing compared to the reception that greeted the film in Germany and Austria, where it was the centre of political controversy and was used effectively by the far Right to further destabilise the elected government.[46]

Universal, it should be said, had been warned. Given the already existing political turmoil, and the way the book had been received, it was inevitable that the film would be controversial in Germany. Carl Laemmle had known from as early as October 1929 that the German nationalists objected to the film. In an interview for the *New York Times* he said: 'The sentiment of the nationalist is so strongly against this book that already … we have been notified by one of the largest theatre chains [in Germany] that they will have nothing to do with the exhibition of such a film in that country.'[47]

However, he was keen to press on: Germany was the second largest market in Europe (there were 5,000 movie theatres in the country); Hollywood relied on European rentals for up to a third of its income; and Laemmle was keen to see the film released in his homeland. Controversy was also good for gaining an audience, as he was later to discover.

Great care had been taken to meet the needs of the German market. During production the Right opposed the making of the film, though it was weak and its influence limited. Nevertheless, Universal were keen to ensure a smooth passage and sought advice from the Studio Relations Department (SRD), which had been established in 1926 to link companies with state censor bodies.

Although it had no enforcement power until 1930, the SRD knew the censors well, and studios were able to avoid considerable problems if they were consulted first. The MPPDA provided advice throughout, and acted as a liaison point with representatives of the German government in New York and the West Coast.

At first the advice was restricted to the script. The novel was undoubtedly problematic, although the English translation had removed some of the difficulties by taking out questionable aspects of scatology and sex. In February 1930, Colonel Joy, director of the SRD, met with the German consul in San Francisco, Herr Von Hentig, who had already discussed the script with Carl Laemmle. Apart from some technical inaccuracies – customs, dress, habits (which he felt were not significant) – Von Hentig felt that the film could be shown. However, Joy urged caution: 'Herr Von Hentig is an intelligent and cultured German,' he wrote, 'and it is possible that because of these attributes his opinion is not indicative of the average stratum of German intelligence; hence, our desire to make the picture wholly innocuous'.[48] This was good advice.

By this time the political situation had worsened. Rising unemployment had developed into a crisis and a new chancellor, the nationalistic Heinrich Bruening, was appointed. In addition, the government had introduced a bill which banned films showing Germany in a negative light, and *All Quiet on the Western Front* was seen as one such film. Fortunately for Universal the bill had been defeated. Von Hentig was invited to visit once again and, whilst he may have disliked the film personally, he felt that his government would not object.

To ensure a positive reception, Universal prepared a special dubbed edition (Germans have never liked subtitles) with cuts lessening some of the more overt aspects of German militarism. This had been approved by Remarque. The cuts were:

- scene showing recruits diving in the mud a second time
- scene where Himmelstoss is thrashed by troops
- scenes where some soldiers eat ravenously

21. Himmelstoss (John Wray) with Paul Bäumer. One of the controversial sequences deleted in the initial German release (author's collection)

- part of the conversation amongst troops when they talk about the causes of war and where the Kaiser is blamed
- sections relating to the transfer of Kemmerich's boots
- scenes where Himmelstoss goes to the front and is seen to be a coward
- the end of Paul Bäumer's speech to the classroom

This time the film was shown at the German Embassy; apart from some minor changes it was approved.

There was one further hurdle: the German press. Unlike the American critics, most German reviewers – apart, not surprisingly, from those on the Left – gave it the thumbs down. Alfred Hugenberg's media empire led some of the furious attacks on the film (Hugenberg had been a powerful force in Germany for well over a decade). The Nazi daily, *Der Angriff*, called *All Quiet on the Western Front* 'a Jewish lie' and 'a hate film slandering the German soldier'.[49] It was not the merits of the film as cinema that they found difficult (these were generally ignored), it was the politics of the film: as with the book, the anti-war theme was seen as an attack on the German soldier, a portrayal of defeatism and cowardice. The argument that the soldiers represented men of all nations, not Germans, carried little weight. Laemmle had tried, in a cable to newspapers in Berlin, to stress this point, but to no avail.

This special edition failed to satisfy opposition forces who, led by Nazi groups, disrupted the première on the evening of 5 December. By this stage the Nazis were in the ascendancy: their spectacular success in the September 1930 election, where they increased their vote from 2.8 to 18 per cent and won 107 seats in the Reichstag (as against only twelve previously), gave them a strong power base. A disruptive campaign over the film of the book by the hated Remarque, a campaign which could also involve German nationalists who were not Nazis, provided further impetus. Finally, the fact that the publishers and producers of the film were Jewish added extra ammunition, as the cry 'Judenfilm' echoing around the cinema indicated.

During the première, Goebbels made a speech to the audience, stink-bombs and white mice were released and there were riots outside the cinema. Goebbels then led a march of thousands down the fashionable Kurfuerstendamm boulevard. The MPPDA received a cable from their officer on the ground summarising the events of the night: 'Under the leadership of a prominent Reichstag deputy German Fascist fanatics staged an organised demonstration at *All Quiet* last night, compelling suspension of the performance, resulting in street rioting and a serious collision with the police. The entire press, with the exception of the extreme Right, emphatically denounces the Fascist tactics as unwarranted and disgraceful.'[50]

Leni Riefenstahl – who had let Remarque use her apartment to write parts of the book (she later went on to make *Olympia* and *Triumph of the Will* under the Third Reich) – was at the première and talked about it in her autobiography: 'Quite suddenly the theatre was ringing with screams so that at first I thought a fire had started. Panic broke out and girls and women were standing on their seats, shrieking. The film was halted, and it was only when I was out on the street again that I learned from the bystanders that a certain Dr Goebbels, whose name I had never heard before, had caused ... pandemonium.'[51] The campaign continued for five days, even though the press were opposed to it and the police were out in force. (Lewis Milestone may have been present at one of these screenings – he told the FBI that he saw the film in Berlin and had been embarrassed when his presence was announced by the manager and he was greeted with silence.) Demonstrations were then banned.

The political situation continued to worsen. It was not just an economic crisis now; the newly powerful Nazis were flexing their muscles in the Reichstag. Bruening faced a series of no-confidence motions, some of which had attempted to bring down cabinet members linked with the decision to release *All Quiet on the Western Front*. Five German states asked for a review of the original censor's decision (as they were allied to the Right this was hardly surprising) and were successful. On 11 December, only six days after the première, the film was banned by the Supreme Film Censorship Board. The official reasons given were that Germans did not wish to see their own defeat on the screen and the negative portrayal of the German soldier.

Denying that the government had capitulated to mob rule, the German censor, Dr Ernst Seeger, said: 'This film is not a war film but one depicting Germany's defeat, and I should like to see that nation which would tolerate a similar presentation of its downfall.' This point was also made in the official communiqué. It called the film a 'one-sided presentation of war experiences in that it touched only on the war's closing phase, which found the nation starved and exhausted, with fresh recruits made up of the youngest classes'. It added that the film was 'calculated to increase the psychic pressure under which the nation is suffering and also to quicken further existing political and economic conflicts, thereby making it a distinct menace to public order and safety'.[52]

The Nazis were jubilant. *Der Angriff* said 'Victory is ours! We have forced them to their knee[s].'[53] The leaders of the Berlin students' union said: 'Students will not be diverted by such foreign pacifist propaganda from their defence-readiness or their yearning for a free German fatherland.'[54] Some American observers forecast presciently that the events surrounding the film were the beginning of the end for democracy in Germany. The American ambassador, Frederic M. Sackett, cabled his government:

> The suppression of the film version of *All Quiet on the Western Front* has undoubtedly assumed great importance. The National-Socialist Party has succeeded in giving a blow to the prestige of the Government of the Reich, in that it yielded to Nazi compulsion on a clean-cut political issue. ... There is no doubt that this incident has given renewed impetus to the constant and unremitting struggle between the Government and the irreconcilable Opposition, and should the latter eventually succeed in its endeavor to force Dr. Bruening to resign, it may well be found that the present event was a very decided contributive factor in such a result.[55]

The Left and liberal press protested against the decision. The radical *Berliner Tageblatt* said that the ban had been pronounced 'because in Berlin, a city of a million people, a couple of thousand professional loudmouths and political adventurers have artificially staged a storm of indignation ... The only danger facing Germany is not the growth of prattling Nazism, but the laxity, acquiescence and dithering of the so-called bourgeoisie.'[56]

In England, the *Manchester Guardian* was also concerned about the ban and what this exposed about German mentality at this time:

> For years the German Republic has led the world as a land of intellectual freedom. This is no longer so. ... What has

happened now is not merely the suppression of a film ...
nor merely a militarist victory, but a capitulation before the
organized mob, a mob that demonstrated against the world
peace as symbolized by this film, a capitulation that is therefore a betrayal of the world's peace. ... That there is a revival
of German militarist emotion has been clear for some time.
That the force opposed to it is so weak is a startling and
sinister revelation.[57]

In one respect the ban was good for the film: Universal chose to
re-release *All Quiet on the Western Front* in America, where the
crisis ensured news coverage and excellent audiences.

The problems facing the film posed dilemmas for both Universal and the MPPDA: whilst Universal wanted to get the ban
ended, the MPPDA were keen to continue to promote good
links between Hollywood and Germany. The two aims were
mutually exclusive. The Hays Office refused to help, and, whilst
sympathetic, the American ambassador in Germany would act
only on official guidance from the White House, which was not
clear at this time.

Whilst all this was in progress, the film faced new problems in
Austria. As in Germany, political and economic problems were
exploited by Nazi organisations, with the film providing the focus.
After the German ban, *All Quiet on the Western Front* was denounced in the Austrian parliament. Although the government
was powerless to act – censorship was the responsibility of
provincial governments – it decided to recommend that it be
banned. This was not just because of the fear of demonstrations,
it was because the German government had specifically requested
that Austria ban the film. With negotiations under way on a
customs union between the two countries, the Austrian government seemed to have little option but to agree.

At this time Sam Spiegel was Universal's representative in
Berlin.[58] Spiegel was later to find fame as the producer of such
films as *The Bridge on the River Kwai* (1957) and *Lawrence of Arabia*
(1962), though the well-reported difficulties of such films pale

into insignificance when compared to dealing with the Nazis. He got off to a terrible start. His assertion that the US Embassy in Berlin had supported Universal's attempt to end the ban was seen as a lie (which it was), and his view that the US State Department expected no ban in Vienna therefore counted for nothing. He then sacked all Universal staff in Austria and closed the office. If he felt that the Austrian government would cave in to the threat of ending the distribution of Universal's films in Austria, he was mistaken, and provincial censors started to ban the film.

However, the film was not banned by the censors in Vienna, where the distributor had a close relationship with the Social Democratic Party. The planned screening for the trade and media was delayed following protests, but it eventually went ahead on 3 January 1931. The public screening was in jeopardy, however. Following protests from Austrian businesses, the cinema was changed to allow greater crowd control by the police. For two nights 2,000 police faced thousands of Nazi demonstrators. For once the government had thought this through and the location proved difficult for the protesters to reach. It was still very violent, and it was this violence that persuaded the government to ignore the constitution and ban the film. In 1934 Laemmle tried to get the ban lifted and appealed direct to Chancellor Dolfuss. Dolfuss' murder by Nazi forces soon after meant that no further attempts could be made.

Germans were still able to see the film in cinemas across the border in the Netherlands, France and Switzerland, where the German-language version played to full houses, and special trains and buses were provided to meet the large demand. However, Universal were keen to end the ban and began to build links with those on the Left who would support them. The Social Democrats were the largest party in the Reichstag at this stage, but had been effectively gagged by the rise of the Right. The decision by the Nazis to withdraw from the Reichstag in March 1931 led to the Social Democrats ending the ban. Universal were satisfied.

However, the American government was not. Fearing further demonstrations and political instability, and concerned about the loss of the German market, the government wanted a delay. This was agreed.

By September 1931 the position had stabilised and Bruening's cabinet felt more secure. Universal felt that the German market could still be tapped and, if the ban were lifted, it would be rescinded in Austria as well. There was still a feeling of desperation, though: to get the ban removed, Universal agreed to prepare a new print which would become the official version for future worldwide release (the Germans wanted few deletions, apparently). Albert Einstein was one of the intellectuals supporting the exhibition of the film. The release led to some protests, but no violence, and it did good, if not spectacular, business. The film was banned again on Hitler's accession to power and was not seen until April 1952, when it attracted large audiences. There was no attempt to reconstruct the original version, or even the cut German edition, until much later, however.

German influence continued to bear down on the film during the 1930s. At some point between 1934 and 1938 the film was banned in Shanghai. An undated report in MPPDA files states: 'We have always had considerable trouble with this picture … Now … [it] is BANNED in its entirety, which prohibits its showing in the settlement and French Concession. This ban is the result of an unfavourable report by the Police Censors and of the objection raised by the local German community.'[59]

German memories were certainly long, as Lew Ayres discovered on a visit he made to Germany in the mid-1930s. 'When I went in 1936,' he said 'I travelled on this beautiful big ship – the *Bremen*. It was my first trip and there was … of course, a German crew. And when they found out that I had been in *All Quiet on the Western Front* some of them came to me and told me that it was a terrible picture and that no one should see … [it] because it was all false. And I felt very bad about it.'[60] Carl Laemmle also had problems: he liked to visit Laupheim each year, but the problems with the film meant that he was not to see his place of birth again.

One of the myths associated with *All Quiet on the Western Front* is that it was banned in France and not shown there until 1962. The truth is that the film was shown publicly in its original censored release right through to 1939. It was a great success. This is not surprising: of all European countries France was the one most sympathetic to pacifism at this time.

This was not without difficulty, though. Having seen the script, Valentine Mandelstamm, a representative of the government (who wanted the film shown) wrote to Carl Laemmle and to Jason Joy requesting that the scene with the French women be deleted. This was not just because of the implication of loose morals:

> The fact that the girls give them sheets to wrap around them-
> selves, does not eliminate the licentious note. But this would
> not be so bad if the women were not shown so terribly low;
> they throw themselves on the food like animals, one of them
> kisses the hand of a German soldier, then there is a concrete
> suggestion – made by showing the empty room – that the
> three men are having an affair with the girls. We hear the
> conversation and we are shown the shadow of a bed, and
> later, when the soldiers have left, we see these girls making
> fun of the men they had just taken on as lovers. ... You say
> that the film is so gruesome that there must be some comedy
> relief. That is true; but it might have been wiser to inject it
> in some other sequence or else to imagine one that would
> be less objectionable.[61]

Mandelstamm warned Laemmle that if the scene was retained, there would be a formal protest from the French government. Moreover, no French audience would accept the storyline. When it was finally submitted, French censors objected to the film and refused to grant a certificate until subtitles had been changed, 'due to the fact that the film portrays the war from the other side'.[62]

The silent version opened in December 1930, the sound presumably soon after, to acclaim and excellent box office. *Variety*'s Paris reviewer said that the film was 'an enormous draw' and that the 'French look upon ... [it] as peace propaganda, and as such, apart from any other quality, give it unstinted praise.'[63] This was shared by French reviewers. One, in *Ciné-Miroir*, said that the film had been made 'with tact, sensitivity and humanity which are of the highest order. It is an absolutely remarkable film, and it deserves to cause a great and legitimate stir in Europe.'[64] According to contemporary reviews there were two scenes missing. The first was the German soldiers' fraternisation with the French women (its inclusion in the book had already caused offence); the second was the removal of parts of the shell-hole sequence where Paul Bäumer stabs Duval.

All Quiet on the Western Front was again banned in late 1939 with the outbreak of war, along with other films which were felt to misrepresent France. In 1963, for the first time (all previous prints had been subtitled), a dubbed version was released.

The release of the film in Norway fomented a wide, spirited, generally favourable, debate. It was shown first in Oslo on 14 March 1931 (the official première was two days later) to a specially invited group. This included members of the Parliamentary Nobel Committee, the government, military officers and representatives of the press. Henrik Soerensen, in the lead front-page article in the newspaper *Dagbladet*, said that everyone in the country should see the film. Complaining that the Nobel Foundation, the Fredsforeningen (Peace Union) and newspapers were asleep on the matter, he advocated free entry for all on Sundays and that all children over twelve should see it. 'Why should war be passed over in silence and lied about?' he said. 'Let all those who are soon to experience the "Western Front" see it. Especially the young ... not just us ... [old people] who will stay at home, take our hats off, tell lies and blow war trumpets.'[65]

Soerensen's article was attacked two days later by Christian

Meyer, Chairman of the Norwegian Navy Association, under the title 'The lie about war'. Taking issue with his pacifism, which he felt was akin to surrender, Meyer said that forcing people to see the film would have no impact on maintaining peace in Europe: 'Had there been many Henrik Soerensens in the country in 1905 and 1914,' he said, 'we might now lack something that Mr Soerensen himself perhaps would not miss: Norway's independent statehood.'[66]

A common criticism (and not just in Norway) was that American accents seemed strange when portraying Germans. *Nationen* was typical: 'The film is set in the German trenches, amongst German soldiers, in German hospitals, in a German village and in a German home,' it said. 'And everyone talks English. The humour, for example, is typically American. It destroys the illusion: you can't help being annoyed by the illogicality of it. The Americans have made an uncommonly good film, and it is not their fault it doesn't ring as true as it could. Let's hope for a German *All Quiet on the Western Front* soon.'[67]

One reviewer, in *Morgenbladet*, disliked the film and praised the German intervention:

> It is easy enough for the *victors* to say that Germany's young men would have been smarter to refuse to go to war, but one has seen enough Anglo-American war stories to know that the tone changes where their own countries are concerned. Then, all the emphasis is on duty: the duty of every man to defend his country. Certainly, war can be terrible, but it is never, never meaningless like the war in this film. It only shows us what we already know: that even the most imperialist country can testify with conviction to the blessings of peace when it is preaching to others.

He added:

> As for trying to hold up the film as a picture of morale ... in the German Army, even at the time of greatest despair: that is monstrous, and the falsehood is obvious to anyone

with the slightest knowledge of what actually happened. The way the troops returned home after the Armistice in excellent order – through a country torn by revolt and deprivation – is sufficient proof of that army's great mental strength and excellent discipline, which, under those conditions, must have depended more than ever before on the troops' trust in and respect for their leaders and officers. That American film-makers know what it pays to produce, and act accordingly, is only reasonable, but it is equally reasonable for the sensible and patriotic segment of the German population to protest against a picture which is distorted and, on substantial points, false.[68]

All Quiet on the Western Front was banned at times in China, Yugoslavia, Hungary and Bulgaria and was never shown publicly in the Soviet Union. The film was also cut in Prague (the scene with Duval, and unidentified scenes portraying suffering in the trenches – not much was left, presumably); in Singapore (similar deletions, but in addition parts of the scene with the French women) and in Poland, where the heaviest cuts of all were made. According to MPPDA records, *all* of the following were cut: Bäumer with Duval, the boys with the French women and Bäumer's return to school. Also missing from the Polish release was Bäumer's death. This must have made for a very confusing film, and audiences must have felt short-changed not to have the ending explained.

The film had problems also in Italy. Mussolini had already banned the book. Sam Spiegel, according to his biographer (in a poor biography), gave the Fascist a private view of the film in his villa. Spiegel said that, surprisingly, Mussolini 'liked the film' and 'he congratulated Universal and me, and said it was the greatest film he had ever seen'.[69] However, it did not fit with Mussolini's political outlook and was banned. Andrew Sinclair said that Spiegel also showed the film to the delegates at the Geneva World Disarmament Conference.[70]

By this time, late 1931, the initial release of the film worldwide had ended. Within twelve months, *All Quiet on the Western Front* had been praised and vilified, attracted massive audiences and fomented political crises in two countries. The critical reception at home had been good, which must have pleased the studio; but what must they have thought about the violence and controversy which their film had generated?

This is not the end of the story of *All Quiet on the Western Front*. The film has been re-released many times over the past sixty-seven years, and each release was associated with debate and controversy. The two other books in Remarque's trilogy were also filmed in the 1930s, and each was acclaimed, condemned, censored and banned. The next chapter covers the continuing sorry tale of *All Quiet on the Western Front*, as well as the filming of *The Road Back* and *Three Comrades*.

6

The Aftermath: *The Road Back,* *Three Comrades* and *All Quiet on* *the Western Front* (1932–1997)

So what would have followed Bäumer's death? In real life, Mrs Bäumer, frightened and dying, would have received a letter informing her of Paul's death. It would have been written by someone tired – tired of the war and of the letters and telegrams he had sent saying how bravely her boy had fought, and what little suffering there had been at the end. Even someone as compassionate as Wilfred Owen could not keep up the pretence for the duration of the war. 'My senses are charred,' he said. 'I don't take the cigarette out of my mouth when I write Deceased over their letters.'[1]

What, however, would have happened if Paul Bäumer had lived? He would have returned to Germany a broken man, as so many did, humiliated, bitter at the folly his country had pursued and distraught at the loss of his friends. Few would have cared, or understood, and there was nothing that they could do. As Paul Bäumer had said in the novel:

> Had we returned home in 1916, out of the suffering and
> the strength of our experiences we might have unleashed a

22. The surviving troops celebrate the end of the war in *The Road Back*
(1937) (BFI Films, Posters and Designs)

storm. Now if we go back we will be weary, broken, burnt
out, rootless, and without hope. We will not be able to find
our way anymore. ... And men will not understand us – for
the generation that grew up before us, though it has passed
these years with us already had a home and a calling; now it
will return to its old occupations, and the war will be forgotten – and the generation that has grown up after us will
be strange to us and push us aside. We will be superfluous
even to ourselves, we will grow older, a few will adapt themselves, some others will merely submit, and most will be
bewildered; – the years will pass by and in the end we shall
fall into ruin.[2]

In the light of this, would Bäumer have fulfilled the promise
shown at school of becoming a playwright? Would he have gone

on to find Duval's relatives? It would have made a great sequel. Remarque's trilogy of books about the war were all filmed, and the second, *The Road Back*, dealt with the lives of returning soldiers to Germany (the narrator was Bäumer reborn). But it took many years to make and it was equally controversial.

By then Universal had been taken over in a financial crisis which saw virtually the end of the Laemmles' involvement in the company, and the end of their participation in film-making. There are no accurate income figures for *All Quiet on the Western Front*. It has certainly repaid its investment over the years (probably many times over), but this was not enough at the time to save the Laemmles. In 1930 Universal made a loss of $2.2 million (other studios fared better), and the onset of the Depression saw a radical cost-cutting programme and a change of emphasis in production away from big-budget features. This meant the company could survive for a while (they did better than a number of other studios), but the decision to go ahead with *Showboat* in 1936 was the final straw, and they were taken over by the banks. Carl Laemmle retired and Laemmle Junior left film-making.

Both *The Road Back* and *Three Comrades* addressed the suffering endured by the German people in the 1920s and 1930s. It was, potentially, a great subject for film-makers and writers. D. W. Griffith had already tackled the issue in 1924 with *Isn't Life Wonderful?* However, political instability, and the rise of Hitler, made this a difficult environment in which to portray German life on the American screen. Any attempts were sure to face pressure in Hollywood from the Nazis and their allies, and films released would, along with others from the same company, find it nearly impossible to obtain distribution in many European countries.

That was later. As *All Quiet on the Western Front* was finding considerable success as a book, Universal purchased the rights to *The Road Back* in September 1929. The MPPDA gave a qualified approval to the film in July 1931, and a screenplay was prepared.

In July and August 1932, two further scripts were approved by the MPPDA, but these, and a third submitted the following year, were not produced. Given the problems facing the studio already with *All Quiet on the Western Front*, Universal postponed production and it was to be another four years before *The Road Back* reached the screen. Remarque was to find out that *All Quiet on the Western Front* was not the only book of his to face criticism, interference and censorship during production.

Post-war Germany as a subject for Hollywood did not disappear, however. In early 1932, Paramount released Ernst Lubitsch's *The Man I Killed*, an uncompromising but in many ways gentle attack on the hatred engendered by war. It is undoubtedly a minor masterpiece, though rarely seen now. Few film-makers have matched the sensitivity and care with which Lubitsch brought the emotions of loss, remembrance and contrition to the screen.

The film portrayed German life in 1919, but dealt only tangentially with economic and social despair. Other films were later to address more centrally (though generally not successfully) the unemployment, poverty, and political instability resulting from the war. Lubitsch's theme was more emotional: the need and search for forgiveness. It told the story of Paul Renard who, distraught over having killed Walter Hölderlin during the war, travels to Germany to seek his family's forgiveness. In the end he is able to tell only Walter's fiancé the truth; his parents treat him as their son and their long misery is allayed.

Realising that the prospects of making *The Road Back* had all but disappeared for the present, Universal embarked in 1934 on a low-key treatment of post-war Germany with *Little Man, What Now?*, based on Hans Fallada's best-selling novel, which had been filmed in German the year before (it was a great success). In an enigmatic foreword designed presumably to offset foreign concerns, Carl Laemmle said that his film was a plea for Everyman, who, though suffering, can often find salvation through a woman's love.

Frank Borzage was the director. In 1932 he had made the definitive version of Ernest Hemingway's *A Farewell to Arms*. This had not been a happy experience and, like *All Quiet on the Western Front*, it was censored domestically and internationally. Hemingway's novel was always going to pose difficulties: it was anti-war, it told of the love between an American ambulance-driver and an English nurse (they were not married) and the birth of an illegitimate child, and portrayed the Italian army as corrupt.

Warner Bros. originally planned to take it on, but they dropped the film when the difficulties became too much. Paramount persevered, with considerable investment, but the crude manner in which they dealt with the problems (they had two endings, and tried to show a pretend marriage ceremony) satisfied neither the censors nor Hemingway, who was furious.

Just prior to *Little Man, What Now?*, Borzage had directed *No Greater Glory* for Columbia. This remake of an original German production of 1929 was a symbolic attack on that country's militarism. In the film, young boys learn by playing at war that honour comes to those who die in battle. It was poorly reviewed.

Little Man, What Now? received a better critical reception, based mainly on the quality of the two leads: Margaret Sullavan (as Lammchen) and Douglass Montgomery (Hans Pinneberg). It followed the trials of the two from the discovery that she is pregnant and their ensuing marriage through to the inability of Pinneberg to secure permanent work. The war is left in the background much of the time, even though it is clear that this is responsible for their plight. The film opens with a political rally addressed, though this is unstated, by a leftist group. Indeed, any political comments steer clear of labels – no Communists, Nazis or Socialists are identified – and descriptions about the state of the country are left to a starving couple, who use the terms 'they' and 'we'.

The few references to the war in the film are oblique. When the receptionist for Lammchen's doctor asks Pinneberg about his father, he says he is dead. When asked of what, he replies 'war'.

Later he complains about his low rate of pay. His friend tells him that the world cannot change in a day. Pinneberg's reply is that it did one day in 1914 and blood has been in the air ever since. He does not admit that he is a pacifist but says he is in favour of peace. Pinneberg has been affected greatly by the war. Each time it is mentioned, he falls silent and is deep in thought.

Little Man, What Now? is not a great film, and the lack of any real political comment dilutes its message. Nowadays, it presents a view of pre-Hays Code America: productions that followed could not show a pregnant unmarried woman, and it was probably the last picture for some time to have a couple share a double bed.[3]

Universal reissued *All Quiet on the Western Front* in 1934 in a nine-reel version probably running no longer than 100 minutes, 45 minutes shorter than the original (Carl Laemmle reassured viewers that nothing vital had been removed). The preface was again missing, though a new foreword was added by Laemmle. It said: 'This picture is brought back to you at a time when the whole world is again fearful of war. The story was written by one who hated war because he knew from experience that it is *hell* not *glory*. The mothers of the world will welcome it and will urge their sons to see it. It is greater than mere entertainment, because it is *a war against war itself*. I am intensely proud to offer it to you.'[4] Laemmle said in *Universal Weekly* that he was re-releasing the film because 'there is hardly a spot on the map that is not threatened with war, and because *All Quiet on the Western Front* tells the story of war as it has never been told before in the history of the world'. He also repeated the foreword to the film but added, just prior to the last sentence, 'As a showman and as a hater of legalized murder ... '[5]

The cuts made reflected the concerns of the Germans: there is no revenge attack on Himmelstoss, nor is he seen at the front. Three other scenes were missing – when one of the boys in the classroom imagines the glorious life of a soldier; when Albert and Paul discuss the French poster girl; and the beer-garden scene (almost all the sequence with the French women was included). The reason for these cuts is probably innocent, as they may have been made to make the film short enough to fit a double bill. Universal certainly needed the money: a production recess in 1934 meant that the studio had no new films available and a series of popular products was released (this included *King of Jazz*, in addition to *All Quiet on the Western Front*).

Despite Laemmle's spur to exhibitors – 'Don't book it at all unless you sense its renewed importance at this particular time and [you] can ... back ... it with the kind of campaign you would give a picture just issued for the first time'[6] – it seems to have had little impact at the box office.

In 1936 New Universal resurrected plans to make *The Road Back*. It was not a good time, as Nazi pressure had intensified to the extent that if a studio wished to distribute any of its films in Germany, it had to be careful what it said about the country and its politics. In June 1936 the studio – financially in a difficult position now – resurrected Sherriff's scripts, and James Whale, celebrated director of *Journey's End*, *Frankenstein*, *The Bride of Frankenstein* and *Showboat* (1936), was chosen as director. Universal sent the screenplay to the Production Code Administration (PCA – the powerful censorship body which had been established following campaigns by the Catholic Legion of Decency), whose seal of approval to films was essential if they were to be released.

Initially, Universal accepted that there was little they could do to satisfy the German government, particularly as the film was based on a book by the despised Erich Maria Remarque. In a covering letter to the PCA, the studio stated: 'When this story originally came in four or five years ago, we were loath to produce ... solely due to [the] jeopardy in which its production would have placed our German business at that time.'[7] Nevertheless, careful consideration was given by Universal, the MPPDA, Whale and Sherriff to minimising political controversy. Despite their best efforts, there was no appeasing the Nazis. George Gyssling, the German consul in Los Angeles, wrote to Joseph Breen, Head of West Coast Operations of the MPPDA, when he heard that the film was back in production. He said:

> You probably know, that Mr Carl Laemmle, while he still owned Universal, had shelved this film, realizing that it would, beyond all doubts, lead to controversies and opposition from ... the German government, as the story gives an untrue and distorted picture of the German people. I beg, therefore, to draw your attention to this matter, which has been already discussed at different occasions in former years with representatives of Universal both here and in Berlin, so you may use your influence on behalf of current relations between the American film industry and Germany.[8]

Breen wrote to Charles R. Rogers of Universal in October 1936 saying that the screenplay met Production Code requirements but – obviously influenced by Gyssling – suggested that the studio consult its foreign department 'as to the acceptability of this picture abroad, in view of its powerful antimilitaristic flavor, as it is more than possible that a picture based on this book will be rejected by a number of political censor boards, particularly outside of this country.'[9] By this stage, however, the German market was limited; indeed, Universal had virtually given up and had recalled Joe Pasternak, their representative in Germany. Rogers knew that *The Road Back* would be banned in Germany and elsewhere, but was confident that the anti-war nature of the film would be popular and make money in the United States and in Britain. What he did not predict was that there would be protests against actual production.

On 9 April 1937, Gyssling wrote to all the leading cast players, technical staff, and Universal executives warning them that if they persisted with the production, all films they were associated with could be banned in his country: 'With reference to the picture *The Road Back*, in which you are said to play a part,' he wrote, 'I have been instructed by my government to issue to you a warning in accordance with article 15 of the German decree of June 28, 1932, regulating the exhibition of foreign motion picture films. ... You will note that the allocation of permits may be refused for films with which persons are connected, who have already participated in the production of pictures detrimental to German prestige.'[10]

The response was swift. Whale said 'Fuck those Germans!'; one actor wanted to punch Gyssling 'in the fucking nose',[11] and another complained to the State Department and asked them to 'advise me whether, as a citizen of the United States, it in the future will be incumbent upon me in seeking my livelihood to yield to the pressure which is brought to bear upon me by a foreign consul, acting under his exequatur and upon instructions of his government, or whether I can look [to you] for protection.'[12] Complaints from the State Department (following protests from the Hollywood Anti-Nazi League and the Screen Actors Guild) led to an apology, but Gyssling continued to intervene. He was eventually told to stop by the German government (he said he had simply been following orders from Berlin) and the German ambassador later apologised.

The film that resulted proved to be a travesty of the original book and the early scripts. Many anti-war points were removed prior to release, and comic scenes either embellished or added. It was also marred by inappropriate casting – in particular John King, who was ineffectual as the lead character – and by a difficult production which led to cost overruns (the film was $200,000 over budget by the end).

Most critics accepted that the film was mixed, and it is true that there remain, after all the problems, some moments which are astounding pieces of cinema. The battle scene on the night of 10 November is filmed with power, and highlights all the brutality and waste of war. *Life* called these twelve minutes 'the most cruel war scenes ever filmed by Hollywood'.[13] Another brilliant moment takes place after the war is over, when the few remaining members of the battalion line up, and around them form the ghostly figures of the dead. This was reminiscent of Milestone's ending to *All Quiet on the Western Front*.

The Road Back opens with the war-weary soldiers in the trenches on 10 November 1918. The experienced, cynical Tjaden (the only remaining member of the company portrayed in *All Quiet on the Western Front*) tells his comrades that the war will never end. Max Weil (Larry Blake) argues that the soldiers have to end it themselves. That night they are ordered to attack an enemy target, and half the company are killed, many are wounded, and one is driven insane.

The next day the Armistice is signed and the company – happy that war is now over – travel back home. They are greeted by revolutionaries demanding that they tear off their military insignia. They refuse and a fight develops which is only stopped when Willy (Andy Devine) threatens them with a mock grenade. It is difficult for them to find peace back home and school means nothing to them now.

The streets are filled with revolutionaries and angry groups attack the town hall. Weil tries to stop the troops firing at the people but is gunned down on the orders of his old commander, Von Hagen (John Emery). Meanwhile, Albert (Maurice Murphy) finds that Lucy, his wife, (Barbara Read) has been having an affair with Bartscher (William B. Davidson), a war profiteer. One night Albert shoots Bartscher. Later he is found guilty of murder, despite the efforts of his comrades to defend his action.

The original screenplay ends with some of the soldiers walking in a forest after the conviction. There they encounter, to their disgust, a dwarf in military uniform drilling schoolboys for another war. Facing considerable financial pressure, and now wanting to pursue any method to satisfy the Germans (they owned real estate in Germany with a value of $450,000, so any revival of the foreign market would have been welcome), Universal substituted a montage of troops of all nations for this ending and insisted on a further twenty changes to lighten the tone of the film. Whale hated the Nazis, refused to cooperate and was replaced as

23. The original ending for *The Road Back* (1937) (Wisconsin Center for Film and Theater Studies)

director for the additional scenes by Ted Sloman, ironically an English Jew. According to *Variety* – under the heading 'U Cuts *Road Back* for Nazi Ambassador's Okay' – the cuts had been made to 'cultivate the good will of Germany'.[14]

Even such an emasculated version failed to satisfy the Germans. Universal offered a pre-release viewing to Hans Luther, the ambassador in New York, but he refused to participate. His successor said later that as he had no right to intervene or pass judgement on such a matter it would have been inappropriate to attend. The film was eventually banned in Greece, China and Brazil, following pressure from the respective German consuls.

Surprisingly, *The Road Back* enjoyed some positive notices, and initially broke box office records, although it had a poor reception in New York. In marketing, *The Road Back* was portrayed as 'big brother of *All Quiet on the Western Front*'. *Life* made it its movie of the week. *Cue* said that James Whale had brought a 'genuinely moving film' to the screen which was 'superb anti-war propaganda',[15] and Louella Parsons said that it 'stirs the heart as well as the mind!'[16]

Some reviewers pointed to the pressure placed on the studio during production. The *Hollywood Spectator* called the film a magnificent achievement, but said that it was 'a pale shadow of what it could have been if the cutter's shears had not been wielded so cruelly'.[17] The fastidious Frank Nugent in the *New York Times* pointed to the central problem in the production: 'It is Universal's *The Road Back*, not Erich Maria Remarque's, that they presented last night at the Globe,' he said. 'It is an approximation of the novel; it is touched occasionally with the author's bleak spirit. But most of the time, it goes its own Hollywoodean-headed way, playing up the comedy, melodramatizing rather than dramatizing.'[18]

Nugent said he had gone back to the original novel and screenplay to understand the film. Knowing little about the backlot machinations, he felt that Universal had misunderstood the story. The studio 'has narrowed it and cheapened it and made it pointless,' he concluded.[19] Unsurprisingly, it was reported that Remarque did not like the film.

As expected, *The Road Back* was not distributed in Germany, but it did achieve some success in Britain despite a poor critical reception. Graham Greene called it awful: 'one big Mother's Day, celebrated by American youth, plump, adolescent faces with breaking sissy voices. Voices which began to break in the trenches … are still breaking an hour and a quarter later … We've lived through a lot in that time, but not through war, revolution, [and] starvation.'[20]

Film Weekly was equally dismissive. 'What was originally intended as a powerful sermon on the horrors of the aftermath of war in a defeated country', it said, 'has become a sketchy story of one or two personal affairs, punctuated with larger sequences which fail to epitomise community unrest and disillusionment.'[21]

The *Monthly Film Bulletin* said that most viewers would be unlikely 'to be very sympathetic to ... [war's] victims, as they are portrayed in this film'. However, their reviewer found that parts were humorous and the riot sequence was well shot.[22] *Time* summed up the problem: 'By mixing fury and farce, Director Whale imperils Author Remarque's poignant theme, but the screenplay possesses intense, impressive street scenes. And for a few moments, *The Road Back* illumines a grim war-racked civilization, lighting up in a final flash the reawakening of German military mania.'[23]

The film of the third volume of Remarque's trilogy about the First World War – *Three Comrades* – was released by MGM the following year. Although Frank Borzage directed a generally faithful adaptation (replacing the cohabiting couple in the book with a husband and wife), the experience of *The Road Back* spurred censors and studio executives again to reduce political content to a minimum.

Indeed, the MPPDA advised that it might be best not to commence production at all. In January 1938 Joseph Breen wrote to Louis B. Mayer arguing that any film of this nature would lead to protests from the Nazis and German-Americans, and would almost certainly be banned in Italy. Furthermore, it would place in jeopardy MGM's business interests in Germany. Breen went on to say that a careful revision of the screenplay might help, but this would be unlikely to lessen the violent resentment that would inevitably result. Finally, he appealed for restraint on the grounds that it would not be just MGM that suffered, but the whole cinema industry.

The MPPDA's entreaties did not stop MGM entering *Three Comrades* into production. Breen, still concerned, held a meeting with various studio staff and the producer, Joseph Mankiewicz, at which various amendments were made to the screenplay. They all agreed that the film would establish clearly that the story is taking place in the period 1918–20, so that no association could be made with the Nazis, and any dialogue or visual references to democracy, book burnings, emblems, and political parties were taken out. It was reported later by the radical journal *New Masses* that, to offset further problems, Breen had suggested that any agitators pictured could be Communists rather than Nazis, and that references to uniformed thugs and attacks on Jews be discarded.[24]

Mankiewicz refused to implement the advice on the Communists, earning a hug and a kiss from a much discontented Scott Fitzgerald, whose first screenplay for the production had encountered considerable criticism.[25] Other suggested changes were incorporated, however. In addition, George Gyssling saw an advance copy of the film, and suggestions from that viewing – whether they were the MPPDA's or the consul's is not clear – were all accepted. These included the cutting of a shot of drums heading a parade, a shortening of a riot scene, and reductions to a fist-fight over a car crash.

This whole experience proved difficult for Mankiewicz, who was not only the producer of the film but a member of MGM's executive committee. Earlier he had been MGM's liaison officer with German speakers arriving in the country, and was very critical of his studio's attitude towards the Nazis. He said later that MGM continued to distribute films in Germany after other companies had either been banned or launched their own boycott. 'Warner Brothers had guts,' he commented. 'They hated the Nazis more than they cared for the German grosses. MGM did not. It kept on releasing its films in Nazi Germany until Hitler finally threw them out. In fact, one producer was in charge of taking anyone's name off a picture's credits if it sounded Jewish.'[26]

Remarque wanted *Three Comrades*, like *The Road Back*, to show the misery and despair faced by returning veterans and the suffering of German citizens caused by the war. In an early section of the book, Bobby, the lead character (Erich in the film), contemplates his and his comrades' lives since 1918. 'We had meant to wage war against the lies, the selfishness, the greed, the inertia of the heart that was the cause of all that lay behind us ... ', he thinks. He continues: 'we had become hard, without trust in anything but in our comrades beside us and in things, the sky, trees, the earth, bread, tobacco, that never played false to any man – and what had come of it? All collapsed, perverted and forgotten. And to those who had not forgotten was left only powerlessness, despair, indifference and schnapps. The day of great dreams for the future of mankind was past. The busybodies, the self-seekers triumphed.'[27]

Shorn of much of its social and political comment, the film turned out to be less depressing, and concentrated on the book's main narrative of a love story between the two leads, Pat Hollmann (played by Margaret Sullavan) and Erich Lohkamp (Robert Taylor).

Lohkamp, along with his two army friends, Otto Koster (Franchot Tone) and Gottfried Lenz (Robert Young), return from the front to find political instability and no work, as their garage attracts little business. One day they meet Pat driving in the country, and, encouraged by the others, Erich invites her out. The two fall in love and get married. Unfortunately, the tuberculosis she has suffered from previously reasserts itself on their honeymoon, and she is ordered to go to a sanatorium for the winter.

She is late in going, but once there she is advised to have an operation which may cure her for good. Meanwhile, back in the city, Gottfried is shot as he helps an old comrade to safety after mobs attack him. Later, Otto obtains revenge by assassinating the murderer.

This news is kept from Pat, but she guesses when Gottfried fails to visit. The operation takes place and she is ordered to rest. Realising that she has placed an intolerable financial and mental burden on Erich and Otto she sacrifices herself by leaving her bed and walking to the window to see them say goodbye. The films ends with the two men leaving the graves of their comrades as they set off for South America. As they depart, gunfire is heard in the city.

Three Comrades is not a bad film overall, although there seems

24. Margaret Sullavan and Robert Taylor, stars of *Three Comrades* (1938)
(BFI Stills, Posters and Designs)

little point to the exercise. Pat's sacrifice, without knowing the results of the operation, seems foolish (in the book there is no operation as her illness is too advanced). Furthermore, whilst South America is seen as a panacea for their troubles, the reason for this is never explained, except that one of the characters has worked there before. It is ironic to think that after 1945 the region became notorious for harbouring Nazi war criminals.

The major difficulty, particularly for those who knew the book, was the absence of political comment. The one demonstration occurs just prior to Gottfried's death, but the speaker uses general statements that have no political reality whatsoever. An additional problem is that, as the MPPDA insisted that the action take place in the two years 1918–20, the film is unable to lay the total blame for Pat's illness and ultimate death on under-nourishment during the war years, which is how Remarque saw it. At one point Pat does say that she grew too tall and ate too little during the conflict and was ill for a year, but this is not presented in the direct manner that Remarque uses in the book. Most viewers would have missed the point. Indeed, they could have assumed that her illness emerged from anywhere, possibly even from extravagant living, as she is a gregarious woman.

Moviegoers were enthusiastic about the film and made it one of the top ten box-office hits of the year. This was helped by the critics, who liked the production and were generous with their praise. They enjoyed particularly Margaret Sullavan, who was awarded the New York Critics' Best Actress Award and the British National Award that year and was nominated also for an Academy Award (she lost to Bette Davis for her stunning portrayal in *Jezebel*). Frank Nugent called it 'a beautiful and memorable film. Faithful to the spirit and, largely, to the letter of the novel, it has been magnificently directed, eloquently written and admirably played ... [O]bviously one of 1938's best ten, and not one to be missed.'[28]

Not all critics were so voluble with their praise. *Newsweek* lamented the removal of much of the social and political aspects: 'Pat, brought vividly to life by Miss Sullavan, dominates the film and gives it its chief claim to reality. ... In the novel Remarque also allows Pat to dominate, but her tragic romance is plotted against a background of hunger, despair, and political turmoil. In attempting to capture a cautious minimum of that unrest for the film, Frank Borzage ... succeeds only in confusing a sometimes poignant love story.'[29]

Finally, *Variety* was also critical, though ultimately wrong in its prediction of its commercial impact. 'Just what Frank Borzage is trying to prove ... is very difficult to fathom from watching the confusing performances of [the leads] ... There must have been some reason for making this picture, but it certainly isn't in the cause of entertainment. It provides a dull interlude.' It concluded: 'despite all the draught of the star names, it's in for a sharp nose-dive at the box office. ... Borzage is off on the wrong foot this time.'[30]

Nazi attacks on Hollywood continued after 1938. *Confessions of a Nazi Spy* (1939), *The Great Dictator* (1940) and *The Mortal Storm* (1940), amongst others, all attracted criticism. By this stage the Second World War had started, and with America officially neutral there was no repeat of the pressure exerted earlier.

The *All Quiet on the Western Front* saga continued in 1939 with the most remarkable re-release of them all. This included an anti-Nazi, anti-war commentary (the narration was written by Gordon Kahn, later to be one of the Hollywood Ten, and spoken by John Deering with a booming, hectoring voice in *March of Time* style). Two new reels were added at the beginning and end with news footage covering the First World War and the rise of Nazism. The rest was the 1934 release version, which had suffered substantial cuts (the full text of the narration is contained in the appendix).

This was undoubtedly released to cash in on the outbreak of war. But there was also a wish to keep America out of a second European war. Near the end of the first reel, the narrator states: '*All Quiet on the Western Front* is shown again to help reassay the human values that keep us within the bounds of watchful peace. It is more than a privilege, it is our sacred duty at this time, to again present *All Quiet on the Western Front* – and to retell in terms of today the bitter lessons of yesterday. It is our contribution to the prayers of all our people – that there shall be *no* blackout of peace in America!'[31]

Of all their many tamperings with *All Quiet on the Western Front*, Universal should be most embarrassed by this version. Disingenuously, and shamelessly, they portrayed this print in their publicity as the full version and recommended that the following 105 words should be at the heart of any advertising campaign (there are only 105 words if the asterisks and exclamation marks are included):

* The guns spew again!
* Men are mad again!
* The world faces a crimson hell again —
* Therefore ...
  TRUTH MUST LIVE AGAIN!
* The book was burned
* The picture was banned
* The author was exiled
* BUT YOU CAN'T
  BLACKOUT TRUTH!
* At last!
  THE UNCENSORED
     VERSION of
       'ALL QUIET ON THE WESTERN FRONT'
  from Erich Maria Remarque's timeless book
* Timelier than ever!
* More Vital Than The Very Breath You Are Drawing Now!
* It is a privilege and a duty to present it
* It is a duty and lifelong revelation to see it!

Universal suggested that exhibitors should use the new war to sell the old, with military maps placed in foyers and – so that all angles were covered – to approach military, patriotic and peace organisations for ticket sales.

Some critics were taken in by the hype (and by the strength of the film that remained), praising, as the reviewer in *Commonweal* did, the film's terrific 'force in its argument against war's futility'.[32] *Newsweek* said that despite sacrificing 'some of its dramatic effectiveness in the interest of a superficial timeliness ... this sympathetic story retains much of the original's bitter denunciation of war.'[33] Others were not so taken, however. *Time* condemned the film:

> When Carl Laemmle Jr. produced this picture in 1930, critics hailed it as one of the few great U. S. films ... But its conscientious producers tried to improve the masterpiece ... When the revamped picture opened, [the] result of such tinkering was almost as complete a disaster for *All Quiet on the Western Front* as even Nazis could have wished. Hard to spot were any restored cuts. The historical newsreel was a separate show. The strident commentator, harshly sounding off in the worst tradition of Russian soap-box films, demolished each of the picture's high-voltage moving climaxes as efficiently as if a 12-inch shell had ripped through the screen.[34]

And Frank Nugent commented in the *New York Times*: 'That it isn't as good a film this way, that it comes, in fact, closer to stupid vandalism – and what can be more stupid than mutilation of one's own art treasures? – is merely a personal opinion. I've no doubt a number of filmgoers will find that its semi-documentary beginning and close, its narrator's fuller explanation service lend it topical significance and patriotic fervour ... but we should have preferred seeing it as it was before it went through its second battle on Hollywood's western front.'[35]

Of all the versions released of his film, Lewis Milestone hated this one, calling it a horror: 'It was produced by an element that was most anxious to spread the word that "The Yanks were not coming," just before they did come. The slogan was of course doomed to failure, as was that version.' He said that it was pulled from distribution very quickly.[36] (Also in 1939 Joseph Goebbels watched again *All Quiet on the Western Front* in his private cinema. He clearly liked the film, despite all his efforts to destroy it.)

All Quiet on the Western Front was not the only film to suffer such indignity. Universal also released *The Road Back*, again with a narration written by Gordon Kahn and spoken by John Deering. As with Milestone's film, Universal declared in pre-publicity, and in the narration itself, that this was the full, uncensored version. Indeed, with bare-faced cheek, they claimed that new scenes that were prevented at the time from being made had been added. Like its more illustrious predecessor, however, it was actually cut further, with the only additions being montage sections placed at the beginning and end, and a brief scene portraying Hitler in a beer-cellar addressing his small group of supporters. Ironically, the dictator was played by Larry Blake, who had portrayed the radical Socialist soldier in the original film. This was the first fictional appearance by Hitler on the American screen.

This period of Hollywood history – when business interests and profits prevailed over morality – proved to be a time of shame, although it differed little from most other responses to the growing Nazi menace in Europe. The débâcle of *All Quiet on the Western Front* in Germany proved to be the catalyst. When Universal agreed to cut the film worldwide to satisfy the Nazis, they had opened themselves up to future interference. Any attempt to film another Remarque novel (particularly a continuation of the first story) was bound to face trouble. Given the problems they had faced already, it was incredible both that Universal bothered at all to make *The Road Back* and, after taking such a decision, that they should have acquiesced further.

The film that was released proved not to be the sequel that critics and others had expected. In a sense it was unnecessary. A continuation of the story had appeared already with *The Man I Killed*. Although it reversed the nationalities of the lead characters, Lubitsch carried over many of the themes (and lives) explored in Milestone's film. If he had survived, Paul Bäumer would have been like Paul Renard: distraught at having killed Gerard Duval, he would have gone in search of the latter's family to seek forgiveness and help them face the future. Even if, like Renard, he was unable to tell the truth, his presence would have brought music and love back into their lives.

All Quiet on the Western Front was re-released again in 1950, and then reconstructed in 1984 in Germany, in the 1990s in Holland and Germany, and a new reconstruction was underway in 1997 in the United States. The 1950 release coincided with the Korean War and came in the midst of the Cold War. This was basically the 1934 version with, curiously, a swing sound-track replacing the solemn music at the end (one German commentator has said that, as the United States was at war, this was done to avoid too downbeat an end[37]). The context was not lost on contemporary reviewers.

The New York *Herald Tribune* (one of many reviews to make this point) said that there was: 'a curious timing in its re-release at this moment. There is nothing equivocal about the message of *All Quiet on the Western Front*: it argues the horror and futility of war both in words and in action. It points up the tremendous gulf between cause and effect, between considerations of international policy and the individual suffering that is their result.'[38]

Universal went all-out on publicity and, as in 1939, claimed that this was the restored version. This impressed reviewers. The *Herald Tribune* continued their review: '[the film] has never before been publicly revived in this, its original form. Since its first Academy Award release in 1930 it has been subjected to heavy censorship in various parts of the world and has been seen over the years in differing versions. However, all the cut footage has been put back together again.'[39]

The fact that this version ran forty minutes shorter than the original release shows how little was now known about the original film amongst Hollywood critics, and how successful studio publicity can be.

In 1950, *All Quiet on the Western Front* was blacklisted by the United States Information Agency with eighty-one other movies (these included *All the King's Men* and *Sweet Smell of Success*). The reason, this time, was economic as well as political. Some film companies had taken advantage of a government convertability programme which, by exhibiting films, allowed them to convert blocked foreign currency into dollars. This was not too serious, as the countries affected offered limited revenue (there were twelve, including Burma, Chile, Poland, Spain and Vietnam), but the fact that some politicians objected to what they felt the films said about America showed that *All Quiet on the Western Front* had lost none of its power.[40]

In the 1960s, *All Quiet on the Western Front* was one of the films considered for colourisation and conversion to a widescreen format. *Variety* reported in 1967 that Universal was the only studio experimenting with turning black and white into colour and, at a cost of between $100,000 and $200,000 Milestone's film was being transferred. The idea was dropped, however.

More promising was the widescreen proposal. MGM's success in putting *Gone With the Wind* into a widescreen format prompted Universal to consider doing the same for *All Quiet on the Western Front*, and work took place in Japan to hand-colour the print and to re-record the soundtrack in stereo. However, the technology was not advanced enough at this stage. In addition, a poor negative and soundtrack meant that this idea, too, was dropped. Universal feared also that the film would not be well enough known to justify release.[41]

All Quiet on the Western Front was remade in 1979 in a generally pointless production. It was directed by the veteran film-maker Delbert Mann – prior to this he had made such films as *Marty* (1955), which had won an Academy Award, and *The Dark at the Top of the Stairs* (1960), before going on to make television films. Paul Bäumer was played by Richard Thomas, and Kat by Ernest Borgnine. Although this was a faithful adaptation of the book, it lacked the power and the emotion of Milestone's film. Thomas

– famous for his role as John Boy Walton in the long-running American bucolic soap, *The Waltons* – was no Ayres. Whilst Borgnine was better, no one could have replaced Wolheim.

It was poorly reviewed and sank quickly. Nigel Andrews in the *Financial Times* called it a 'terminally torpid remake', and said that it 'sprawls over 127 minutes with never a memorable image or a heart-stopping moment'.[42] David Robinson in *The Times* also disliked this new version: 'Mann's detailed naturalism', he said, '... has not half the reality that Milestone's brilliant stylization conveyed. Nor does all the crashing spectacle of battles filmed on Czech locations achieve half the feeling of war that there was in the eerie whines and murmurs that hovered like bird ghosts over Milestone's no-man's-land.'[43]

The film also had the disadvantage of being made in colour, which helped neither story nor cinematography. Trench combat has always been best seen in black and white: monochrome conveys the brutality and the starkness, the sheer awfulness, of the trenches and No Man's Land; colour seems to give it glamour.

The sorry state of *All Quiet on the Western Front* improved somewhat in the 1980s, principally through the work of Jürgen Labenski, a television producer for Germany's broadcasting company, Zweites Deutsches Fernsehen. Using various existing prints, the fullest version yet was reconstructed and shown on German television in 1984 (though the soundtrack was dubbed into German). There is irony here: one of the prints used came from the private collection of that noted cinephile, Joseph Goebbels. Thus it was that history was turned on its head: the man who had done so much to destroy *All Quiet on the Western Front* indirectly contributed to its reconstruction.[44] In the 1990s, two other reconstructions were attempted, the first by Netherlands Television (1993) and the second by Westdeutscher Rundfunk (1995). The German version extends Labenki's reconstruction by including additional footage. It is probably the longest version available. The current video release from United International Pictures is also better. It is still not the full version, but it is nearly there, with most of the key sections that had previously been deleted restored.

By then, Lewis Milestone – and most of those involved – had died (Milestone died in 1980). He would have liked the German version: he had made a near perfect film in 1930, one revered by critics and publics alike, and had seen it cut and savaged and banned. Despite this, he knew that the message he had tried to portray would last. He said in 1964: 'When first released, the film was exactly the way I wanted it ... *All Quiet* had rough sledding in many countries and in some was forbidden exhibition. But I'm glad to report that the picture proved to have a longer life than many a politician and is still going strong in spite of brutal cutting, stupid censors and bigoted politicos.'[45]

The reasons why the film was so powerful, and is still going strong, are explored in Chapter 7.

7

The Greatness and Continuing Significance of *All Quiet on the Western Front*

There are many reasons why *All Quiet on the Western Front* retains its power and has continued to capture the imagination, despite the fact that few have seen a full version and that over half a century of cinema has passed since its first release. It brings together – indeed, helped establish – the classic themes of the anti-war film, book, play and poem: the enemy as comrade; the brutality of militarism; the slaughter of trench warfare; the betrayal of a nation's youth by old men revelling in glory; the incompetence of the High Command; the suffering at home, in particular by women; the dead, and the forgotten men who survived. And it did so in style, without recourse to the romanticism and glorification which marred such war films as *The Big Parade*.

All Quiet on the Western Front was a leap forward for cinema in critically addressing war and peace issues. Here the Great War is seen as it was: a brutal waste. No film up to then had shown this – indeed, had *been able* to show this as the time was not right and the camera was incapable, in the early sound era, of re-creating the reality of trench combat. Only *Paths of Glory* has since been

25. Paul Bäumer with Gerard Duval (Raymond Griffith). Duval's death, and Bäumer's response, showed the futility of war and nationalism (author's collection)

able to capture the terror of war, the waiting for the attack, the inevitability of death.

In its attack on militarism, *All Quiet on the Western Front* was telling millions what the great war poets had stated so eloquently, and with its own eloquence. A. P. Herbert, in his poem about Gallipoli, spoke for all the dead of the war (*All Quiet on the Western Front* was not about Gallipoli, but the sentiments are the same):

> This is the Fourth of June
> 　Think not I never dream
> The noise of that infernal noon,
> 　The stretchers' endless stream,
> The tales of triumph won,

                   The night that found them lies,
               The wounded wailing in the sun,
                   The dead, the dust, the flies.

               The flies! oh God, the flies,
                   That soiled the sacred dead.
               To see them swarm from dead men's eyes
                   And share the soldiers' bread!
               Nor think I now forget
                   The filth and stench of war,
               The corpses on the parapet,
                   The maggots in the floor.

Apart from what these poets told them, few, even the relatives
of those who had fought and survived, would have been aware
of the *totality* of the suffering of the soldiers in the trenches.
Those who had returned did not – sometimes, owing to disability,
could not – talk about the deaths and injuries they had seen, the
smell of war, the fouling of trousers, the lack of sleep.

All Quiet on the Western Front showed the brutality of war, but
it went further. By saying that the ordinary soldier on one side
was equal to those on the other it provided a message of hope.
Lew Ayres said: '[it] showed the Germans as having the same
values that you and I have ... just people caught in this thing
that's bigger than all of us ... *All Quiet on the Western Front* became
one of the first voices for universality ... [it said] that unity was
possible within the world.'[1]

This was a point Carl Laemmle wished to stress, because he
believed in it and because he felt that it might help offset German
concerns about the film. In his cable to Berlin newspapers during
the political crisis over the film in late 1930, he said that *All Quiet
on the Western Front* 'indicts no nation, no individuals, but ...
records an international human experience'.[2] In the film, Milestone
shows this through the death of Duval, and Bäumer's promise,
never fulfilled, to apologise.

Few soldiers on the battlefield were close enough to the enemy, except in hand-to-hand combat or as prisoners of war, to see this. Fraternisation, where it occurred, was condemned: the rapid ending of the Christmas truce in 1914, when German and British soldiers met in No Man's Land to talk, shake hands and play football, showed how the High Command of both countries were terrified of their men discovering that the enemy wanted peace. Cinema has shown well what can result from an encounter with a representative of the enemy: in *Paths of Glory*, the tired and bitter soldiers recover their humanity when listening to the German girl sing, even though her song is in German; in *La Grande Illusion*, Jean Renoir showed that it was class and not nationality that bound people together, and that ordinary people in different countries had more in common than they at first thought. But it was the meeting between Bäumer and Duval, where they are forced to stay in No Man's Land for days, the Frenchman fatally wounded and Bäumer pleading for forgiveness, that showed how unnecessary the war was.

Betrayal is another key anti-war theme in the film: the boys are betrayed by their teacher, by their fathers and by the High Command. These are the old men of the war – those who forced their boys to fight. Bäumer and his friends are sent away by their teacher (their mentor) and by Himmelstoss. Kantorek is too old to fight, but revenge is sweet for the boys when Himmelstoss arrives at the front. Here he is a coward; his brave words and the military songs of the parade ground are irrelevant. Like the others, he is simply there to die, and for him death comes quickly. The boys also get their own back on Kantorek in the book, when he becomes a member of the reserve army and is forced by one of his ex-pupils to do parade duty. In the film the condemnation is more direct when Bäumer returns to the classroom and condemns Kantorek.

The incompetence of the High Command, in a war where military ineptitude was a daily event, was another common theme in the best anti-war cinema. The culmination of this point of view in cinema can be seen in *Paths of Glory*, the true story of three men executed by firing-squad to hide the mistakes and arrogance of senior officers. This point is not so evident in *All Quiet on the Western Front*, though those behind the lines are criticised. Himmelstoss, the mild postman, is transformed into a sadistic drill sergeant and then found to be a coward at the front; Ginger, the cook, fails to deliver food when the going is rough. Kubrick's film is more direct; perhaps another twenty-five years needed to pass before such bitter thoughts could be put on the screen.

The only social group absent from the film are the politicians, probably the greatest of all liars, who betrayed the troops the most. *Paths of Glory* illustrated this betrayal graphically (Stanley Kubrick has always been interested in power and the abuse of authority, as he has shown in all his films[3]). *All Quiet on the Western Front* did not show this – the focus of condemnation was elsewhere – although the book did include a visit by the Kaiser to the front, where the soldiers benefit from new uniforms.

Unlike many other war films, there is no romanticism of combat in *All Quiet on the Western Front*. Howard Barnes, in his perceptive review of the film in 1930 in the New York *Herald Tribune*, wrote: 'With all preceding war stories brought to the stage or screen ... there has always been an inevitable glamour attaching to fighting, no matter how carefully avoided. ... In *All Quiet* there is no glamour. It is courageously bitter.'[4] Apart from the start, when the teacher sends them away to fight, little is said about the glory of the Fatherland. There are also few women (though, ironically, they were placed centre stage in some publicity – even for such a film, Universal saw the value of attractive women). Those who do appear are there to make a telling point: a brief interlude, tastefully done – though not according to censors at the time – of lovemaking in the midst of horror; and Paul's tortured visit back home to see his dying mother. The scene with the French women is particularly important in stressing the point about the futility of international differences. These were classified as enemies, but there is no animosity between them and the men.

Women rarely had opportunities to appear in anti-war films. It was different in the pro-war film in Hollywood. Here, in such films as *Arms and the Girl*, *The Little American*, *War and the Woman* (all 1917), and *Little Miss Hoover* (1918), women played the daring sister, the exposer of the slacker (particularly if it was a cowardly boyfriend), the brutalised victim, the spy (at home and overseas) and the dutiful wife. The women at home in *All Quiet on the Western Front* are not like this. From the little seen of her, Mrs Bäumer is worried, sick, and dying. Whilst she might come across as simple, and a little naive, she is clearly concerned, as she knows that death is near for her son. And those at the front – the French women – reject national hostility by sleeping with the soldiers.

The coverage of the themes outlined above – and, just as importantly, the way in which they were covered – were all important reasons for the film's success. Another reason is more straightforward: the film was good; it was well made, superbly acted, fast moving, dramatic, emotional. In a collaborative effort, all those involved in *All Quiet on the Western Front* made it the great film that it is: Remarque, for the book without which the film would not exist; the Laemmles with their vision; Edeson with his cinematography; the whole screenwriting team for probably the best script of the early sound period; the technical team for choreographing the battlefields of the war; and the actors and actresses, each of whom play a memorable role, however small. Few films have been as fortunate as *All Quiet on the Western Front* in having such an excellent team.

It was the first film to meet the demands of the sound era, as it succeeded in overcoming the difficulties posed by early sound technology and recreating the mobility of the silent film camera. The director D. W. Griffith said in June 1930: '*All Quiet on the Western Front* is the greatest talkie because it is the most adept combination of the techniques of the old silent films with the new medium of sound and dialogue.'[5] More recently, the film historian David Robinson has praised Milestone's work: 'He brought all the fluidity of silent films to the camera – which freely tracked and panned and soared over the battlefields of the little German town from which the hero and his schoolboy friends march out to war – and to the editing. At the same time Milestone imaginatively explored the possibilities of sound, from the beginning where the bellicose harangues of the schoolteacher are drowned by the noise of a band outside, to the haunting echoes of the battlefield as the cry of "Mind the wire" goes down the line.'[6]

At the end of *All Quiet on the Western Front* most of the boys are dead; as their ghostly figures march away they look directly at the audience, accusing us of sending them to their death, challenging us not to let this happen again. 'To this end you have doomed us',[7] as one reviewer described their thoughts.

The dead, inevitably, featured in many an anti-war film. In *The Road Back* there is an outstanding shot where the company lines up and the few remaining soldiers are joined by the spectres of their comrades. And in Abel Gance's *J'accuse* the dead actually rise up, pleading for justification for their deaths. If the dead could rise they would constitute an army of the betrayed and brutalised carrying an indictment so strong that none could question it.

Those who survived were forgotten – for a time. There were no homes fit for heroes; and jobs were scarce for veterans in the great depression. Anti-war cinema covered the forgotten man creatively: in the musical (the song 'My Forgotten Man' from *Gold Diggers of 1933*) and the gangster movie – *I Am a Fugitive from a Chain Gang* (1932), *They Gave Him a Gun* (1937) and *The Roaring Twenties* (1939) – which took the anti-war message to new audiences. Remarque's books *The Road Back* and *Three Comrades* covered post-war Germany, where the returning soldiers were, in many ways, forgotten men.

The world has remembered, though – and in many ways: the annual Armistice Day commemoration; the creation of war memorials which dot villages, towns and cities in most combatant countries, and the creation of the tomb of the Unknown Soldier. This is an issue covered wonderfully in Bertrand Tavernier's *La Vie et Rien d'Autre – Life and Nothing But* (1989), when the lead is told to find a corpse for burial in the Arc de Triomphe. He has to make sure that the corpse is French, and not British or a Hun. The real memorials for most, though, lie in unmarked graves in the trenches and in No Man's Land, where soldiers died.

In the end it comes down to the fact that the outcome of the First World War was not victory, or glory: it was slaughter and waste. This is the view of the war today, for which *All Quiet on the Western Front* is partly responsible. Did it work? Jean Renoir said that ultimately all the anti-war films about the Great War failed, as a Second World War followed (he said it cynically – the Second World War was a very different war).[8] But they were important then and they remain important today. At a time when warfare and genocide have re-emerged, at the end of this most violent of centuries, there is a continuing need to remember and to warn. In the absence of the personal witness, as most veterans are now dead, the arts provide this service. And as the most popular of the arts, the cinema reaches the widest audience. Out of the thousands of films made about the war, only a few can be described as classics. *All Quiet on the Western Front* is the most important of them all. It comes down through the years with an ever-timely message: where cinema exists, this most disastrous of wars, this appalling waste of a nation's youth, will never be forgotten. It is a memorial – and an ever-present warning – as fitting and honourable as any that grace a village, town or city.

Postscript:
Remarque 1933–1970

At the end of Chapter 6 Erich Maria Remarque was in exile, having fled Nazi Germany in 1933. Like so many of his exiled countrymen, Remarque led the unsettled life of the refugee, staying in a number of countries during the next thirty-seven years with France, Italy, New York and Hollywood all providing him with homes. He was happiest – if he was happy anywhere – in Casa Remarque, his Swiss villa in Ascona, which he had purchased before he left Germany and which he owned at the time of his death. Although unquestionably a difficult time for him, the pain of exile was tempered by his association with other refugees: Thomas Mann and Stefan Zweig were in Ascona; in Hollywood, Remarque joined Fritz Lang, Billy Wilder, Lilli Palmer, Bertolt Brecht, Luise Rainer and many other members of the artistic and literary elite who had escaped Hitler.

He was also wealthy, having managed to remove most of his money from Germany before his accounts had been frozen. He cultivated a playboy image with regular visits to popular holiday destinations and relationships with such glamorous women as Marlene Dietrich, Greta Garbo and Paulette Goddard. He married Goddard in 1958.

Remarque was deprived of his German citizenship in 1938,

although he refused to recognise this, and never applied to have it reinstated. He became an American citizen in 1947. Although he claimed at the time that he no longer had an affinity with Germany, he never lost his love for Osnabrück and the city continued to provide a background for many of his novels. Many years after the war, his homeland did begin slowly to move towards a reconciliation – in July 1967 he was awarded the Distinguished Service Cross of the Order of Merit of the Federal Republic of Germany and a German street was named after his sister the following year – but he continued to resent the way he had been treated. On occasions he returned to Germany, and he went to Osnabrück once, but found the experience traumatic and always returned to Casa Remarque.

He continued to produce work regularly, although he always found writing difficult. Much of his work after 1937 dealt with the experience of exile and the Second World War. Some were good books; none, however, was as good as *All Quiet on the Western Front*. Following *Three Comrades* in 1937, Remarque published *Flotsam* (1941[1]); *Arch of Triumph* (1945), *Spark of Life* (1952), *A Time to Love and a Time to Die* (1954), *The Black Obelisk* (1957), *Heaven Has No Favorites* (1961) and *The Night in Lisbon* (1964). His last novel, *Shadows in Paradise*, was published posthumously in 1972. He also wrote four plays, three of which were staged.

Many of these novels were filmed. *Flotsam*, the story of German refugees and their often futile search for sanctuary, became *So Ends Our Night* in 1941. His original screenplay *Beyond* was made as *The Other Love* in 1947 with David Niven and Barbara Stanwyck. Remarque was reunited with Lewis Milestone the following year with *Arch of Triumph*, the story of the search by a refugee for the Nazi who had tortured him. A large-budget feature, starring Ingrid Bergman, Charles Boyer and Charles Laughton, it was a film of great ambition but a miserable failure. Hollywood versions of *A Time to Love and a Time to Die* – Universal's attempt to create an *All Quiet on the Western Front* for the Second World War, in which Remarque acted (and acted well) – appeared in 1958 and Al Pacino starred in *Bobby Deerfield* (1977), based on his final work *Heaven Has No Favorites*. German television made films of *The Night in Lisbon* (1971) and, eleven years later, *The Black Obelisk* and Polish television broadcast a version of *Arch of Triumph* in 1993. Other television films have been made of Remarque's work.

Remarque died on 25 September 1970. He had been ill for some time. In a bizarre twist, his funeral was attended by hundreds of German tourists, sent there by a tour operator, who thought they would like to see the ceremony.[2] The story of *All Quiet on the Western Front* did not end with his death, however. In December 1995, the handwritten manuscript of an early draft, kept for decades by Jutta Ilse Ingeborg Ellen Zambona, Remarque's first wife (they were actually married and divorced twice), was sold at Sotheby's for £276,500.[3] It was bought by the Niedersächsische Sparkassenstiftung for the Remarque-Archive in Osnabrück. The manuscript includes a new episode containing details of Paul Bäumer's life at home before the war, and there are different names for some of the characters. This unique discovery provides an opportunity for a new, possibly definitive edition of the novel. What is needed now is the release of the full English-language reconstruction of the film.

Appendix:
The 1939 Re-release

The re-release in 1939 of *All Quiet on the Western Front* and *The Road Back* saw a substantial change in the nature of both films. Taking advantage of the outbreak of war, Universal added to each an anti-Nazi, isolationist narration written by Gordon Kahn, better known in the 1950s as a member of the Hollywood Ten, and spoken by John Deering. Reprinted below is the full text of the narration for *All Quiet on the Western Front*.

Reel 1

A new reel has been added at the start with a long exposition on the First World War, the Armistice and the Versailles Treaty, and then the rise of Nazism in Germany. The accompanying visual material corresponds to the subject of the narration. It culminates with a mass book-burning, with *All Quiet on the Western Front* prominent.

Europe 1914 – Echoes of the Balkan Wars still vibrated. The peasant goes back to his acres, content. But there is no content in the chancelleries of the Great Imperialist powers. Only dissatisfaction with the way in which the known world is divided among them. A Serbian fanatic fires a shot. An Austrian Archduke is assassinated and that unleashed the greatest holocaust in the world's history. July – a month of ultimatums. Mobilization! Wheel up the big guns! Armed conflict between Austria and Serbia is imminent, says the world's press. The aged Franz Josef of Austria orders his troops to march. That's just the tinder to the powder barrel. What will the rest of the world do? Cousin Willie Hohenzollern sends an ultimatum to Cousin Nicky Romanoff. Belgium is safe! There is a neutrality treaty – soon destined to become 'a scrap of paper' as Germany goose-steps over the border. France mobilizes! The cries of 'Defend Belgium neutrality!' is drowned out by the clamour to revenge the defeat of 1870. Russia – the bear that walks like a man – staggers over the border of East Prussia. And a million mujiks in uniform are slaughtered in the swamps of Tannenburg. Europe trembles to the roar of new and mighty armament. Italy crosses the high Alps, breaking a neutrality it has maintained for more than a year. England musters her British Expeditionary Force. The German High Command laughs and calls these former clerks and tradesmen 'Kitchener's Contemptibles'. But contemptible or not, they begin swarming across the channel – two million of them! Europe settles down to the grim business of killing. The face of the continent from the North Sea to the Mediterranean is cut with two deep scars as the Entente and the Allies face each other across the corridor that will be forever called No Man's Land. The war brims over into the sea, and in the darkness deep beneath the sea lurks the deadliest engine of terror ever invented by man! The submarine! A better-blockaded Germany orders unrestricted submarine warfare. 'Spur los Versenkt' becomes the German code for 'Sink without trace'. Raiders cruise the seven seas. The ships of no nation are exempt. Millions of tons of shipping go to the bottom. America! Woodrow Wilson is re-elected on the slogan – 'He Kept Us Out of War!' The slogan 'Peace at Any Price' becomes the label of the pacifist. Finally, Germany demands a price that is too great for any people to pay. The *Lusitania*! Eleven hundred men, women and children go down in her hull. And with them go the last pretenses of American neutrality. The Yanks! Vive les Americains! They don't know yet what kind of a fighter the Yank is. Belleau Wood and Château-Thierry show them! The AEF [American Expeditionary Force] fights to within sight of the Rhine. Then, while Germany flames with revolution, Marshal Foch received the enemy's High Command in a secret train in the Forest of Senlis. At last the historic eleventh hour of the eleventh day of the eleventh month of 1918. A bedlam of peace sweeps hysterically over the capitals of the world. Then – a breathing spell to bury the dead and comfort the living before the victors and the vanquished meet – in the Hall of Mirrors. Wilson, the dreamer who wanted peace without victory. Vengeful Clemenceau! The lion-maned Lloyd George, the weak and silent Orlando trace new lines and new borders amputating parts of Germany and grafting them to the bleeding frontiers of other countries. The Versailles Treaty! Hailed as guaranty of eternal peace! Until one day in March 1923 a little band of putschists, led by an obscure Austrian house painter, marches out of a beer hall in Munich shouting a new and fearful battle hymn. He is arrested and thrown into prison, but emerges several years later with the manuscript of a new book – a catalogue of threats and insults. He wins recruits among the dispirited, the hungry and the unemployed. His private army blossoms out in uniforms which give them the right to pillage. His strength grows and German democracy weakens. His dynasty was born in fire – the fire of the Reichstag touched off by his own dupes. And in that profligate blaze that shocked the world the infamous book-burning of 1933! A new, democratic order trying to emerge from the ruins of Germany. But it is betrayed by fierce, unreasoning nationalism that is clubbed into the people by men more merciless than history ever conceived, led by a false messiah and a handful of fanatical apostles. Its creed is – Destroy! Purge! Burn! Paper and ink may vanish in smoke, but when the last book lies in ashes, the flame of bigotry will have nothing to feed upon but itself! You cannot destroy human intellect by fire! You cannot purge ideas! For the second time in our generation the slogan 'The War To End All Wars' is written in human blood. Europe has not profited by the grim example of 1914-1918 that is so graphically portrayed in this picture. Today, when famine, greed, pestilence and death – the Four Horsemen of the Apocalypse – gallop over the face of the continent, *All Quiet on the Western Front* is shown again to help re-assay the human values that keep us within the bounds of watchful peace. It is more than a privilege, it is our sacred duty at this time, to again present *All Quiet on the Western Front* – and to retell in terms of today the bitter lessons of yesterday. It is our contribution to the prayers of all our people – that there shall be *no* blackout of peace in America! We turn back the scroll of history to the Germany of 1914!

Reel 2

As the boys are singing 'The Watch on the Rhine' after deciding to enlist, and through to their arrival on the parade ground:

Once again the poisoned breath of the war-maker extinguishes the lamps of learning. Today, as in 1914, the classrooms of that unhappy country are empty ... but the *trenches* are filled. The athletic fields are silent ... but Flanders Fields throb with the play of the war gods! The student's gown hangs forgotten ... but somebody will have to remember to drape a sheet over his body. But scientific research goes on! More feverishly than ever! Chemists are working twenty-four hour shifts! To fight disease? No! That was yesterday. Today it's to find a poison gas that will leak through the tightest gas mask!

Reel 3

As the bombing of the railway station, where the soldiers are waiting to take the train to move up the line, commences:

The war babies of 1914 are getting their baptism of blood and confirmation by shell-fire in 1939. The tools of war are newer and more efficient then they were then – but their object is the same – to kill the greatest number in the least time!

Shortly after, still with the battle:

The Red Cross for the wounded – the Iron Cross for the survivors – the wooden cross for the dead – and the double cross for all of them!

Reel 4

Following the death of Behm:

They mourned for that boy in 1914. But today mourning is forbidden! There are no published casualty lists. It's unpatriotic! It's bad for civilian morale! No more of those telegrams from the Leader of the State thanking parents for their donation of a son to the greater glory of Nationalism. No more names. Only a number on an identification tag. Grief must become pride – because no mother can tell – maybe it's her son who will be the Unknown Soldier of the second European War!

As troops are in the dugout facing continuous bombardment by the French:

Twenty-five years have passed. The concrete fortification has replaced the dugout. But do the dead and those who are about to die care whether their tombs are mud or marble?

As the battle between the French and Germans continues:

Somewhere in France then, somewhere in Poland *now*. The crash of the barrage is but the curtain-raiser for the Carnival of Death! The signal to attack is the last Sacrament of the Doomed. Shrapnel recognises no brother and high explosive no friend. And now as then, it all adds up to an official communiqué that reads – 'Our troops made a gallant offensive.' A fresh mark on the map and a new medal for the chest of the Generalissimo. Again the night flare shines brighter than the Star of Bethlehem.

Later, with the battle still in progress:

Do you see now why the harvest of 1919 was so abundant? Taken away from his own field, the plowman fell to enrich an alien's vineyards – from which today are being harvested the fruits of hate and multiple murder. Now it's the tired, meager soil of Poland that is being replenished by the same kind of fertilizer. In the First World War a soldier sometimes saw the face of his enemy at bayonet length from his own face before he killed him or was himself killed, but in the streamlined slaughter of today, the warmakers have little use for the bayonet – because a man might notice that the blood on it is the same colour as his own!

Reel 5

At the end of their discussion on the causes of war, and their arrival at the hospital to visit Kemmerich:

Not so loud, soldier! In the war today there are firing squads for soldiers and concentration camps for civilians – who ask too many whys. Why must the vaingloriousness of a war-maker scorch the earth of Europe twice within twenty-five years? Why, in peace terms, human life is priceless, and in war its worth becomes an ounce of lead or six inches of steel? Why the blood of millions must be shed to slake the greedy thirst for power of one man!

Reel 6

As Paul leaves hospital carrying Kemmerich's boots:

There's no lack of boots today for the soldiers' feet. Boots for the goose-step on the parade ground! Boots for the slow minuet of the doomed in a night raid. Boots for the quick-step of the advance – and boots for the last slow shuffle of the retreat. Good boots – and so long as it lasts, good food for his stomach! But those who stay at home must content themselves with ersatz leather and synthetic hopes!

After the death of Duval:

Is there no hope for humanity beyond this? Must man who is made in God's image – forever be the only living thing that mass-murders its own kind? Will he bear the Mark of Cain until even his Maker is impatient of His work? The glorious oaths of yesterday so solemnly sworn in 1919 have been turned into a cruel, pointless joke for the red laughter of the war-gods. The pledge of peace made over the burned cities, the twelve million dead and the millions missing is being redeemed today in the fresh sacrifice of the very orphans of that war. And they who haven't yet begun to live are already marching to death!

Reel 8

In hospital, where Paul is undergoing treatment:

Even today the torch of mercy flickers in the hospitals behind the fight-lines. Here, no enemy is known ... but death. And a can of ether makes all men equal. But what is it at best? A mere service station where the human machine is patched up well enough to be able again to press a trigger.

As a one-legged soldier on crutches crosses Paul's path when he arrives home on leave:

You count the cost of a shattered fortification in the number of broken bodies it cost to take it. Again war decrees a new note in men's fashions. Empty sleeves and wooden legs. Wound stripes and crutches ... the bellow of hunger ... and torment, is back in vogue.

Reel 9

As Paul has finished his speech to the class:

No, Professor, calling a schoolboy an Iron Youth doesn't make him bullet proof. It didn't in 1914 and it won't in 1940. The military bands blending with the siren song of the demagogue in the same savage symphony today that it was then – only the beat is faster. With a swing set to destruction – with a frenzied master of ceremonies calling the tune.

Reel 10

Just after Kat has been found to be dead:

Corporal Stanislaus Katczinsky – Number three o six – multiplied by nine million! Died in action! Died in vain!

Reel 11

At the end of the film as the young dead German soldiers are marching into eternity transposed over the wooden crosses marking the graves of their comrades, another long commentary and sequence was added. Accompanying visual matter starts with the burning of books including *Evolution and Physics* by Albert Einstein, Thomas Mann's *The Magic Mountain*, *Bismarck* by Emil Ludwig and *The Bible*. This is followed by shots of *Mein Kampf* with superimposed shots of Hitler and supporters. Following this is the mobilisation of troops, tanks and aircraft for a new war. Finally, a copy of the book *All Quiet on the Western Front* is seen burning. The commentary goes as follows:

Look backward, you Valiant Dead, at the crosses upon which the great illusions of human brotherhood were crucified. Whose is the guilt? And to whom goes the Glory? Where is the lesson in the parable of your sacrifice? History has spawned a tragic order under which the noblest thoughts of man and the Word of God are expunged by fire and blood. An evil day saw a fanatical testament rise out of this pyre. The world read and was alarmed. Other nations comforted themselves by saying, 'It can't happen!' There are treaties – pacts and solemn promises. There's the German people. But a people sick of their war wounds are easy recruits to any ideology that promises bread and shelter. And those that did not agree felt the rubber bludgeons – the concentration camps – the purge or were driven to exile. To those who remained it was, 'Fall into the lock-step! Conform or die!' March – you sons and brothers of the fallen on the Western Front. Tighten up your belts and march! *Mein Kampf* promised good, white bread for you in the Ukraine! Butter and milk in Poland and Roumania! 'Carry spades, for soon there will be rifles enough for all!' says *Mein Kampf*. 'The Aryan Man is Master of Creation. All others are corrupt races. And if that is lunacy, then lunacy becomes us!' is the challenge. The state is the Alpha and Omega! The All in All! The Leader is the State and every living soul must wear its livery. And that means *every living soul!* Bluster becomes action! And before the shock of one act was fully realised – another was committed! The Treaty of Versailles became a dead letter! In defiance of covenants the greatest military force in German history was mustered! Tanks were forbidden. But they rolled across the border into Austria. The Rhineland must remain demilitarized! But the Siegfried Line is no child's sandpile! Only sports planes was the promise given. Yet today – ten thousand fighting machines were aloft and a thousand more a month are being built! Every threat made in the pages of *Mein Kampf* was carried out. But the first promise is yet to be carried out. Austria! The Sudetenland! Czechoslovakia! Memel! Today Danzig! Tomorrow the Corridor. One challenge too many, and the 'War of Nerves' flares into another 'War To End All Wars!' The mud of Poland seethes with the 'blitzkrieg' of the Invader. And again in the crimson deadlock of another great war – while civilization hangs on the outcome – fresh millions hurry to their rendezvous with Fate while the Congress of the Dead meets where ALL'S QUIET ON THE WESTERN FRONT.

Notes

Introduction

1. See Sassoon's poem from 1920, 'Picture Show', in A. Slide, ed., *The Picture Dancing on the Screen: poetry of the cinema*, New York, The Vestal Press, nd, p. 26.
2. W. Percy, *The Moviegoer*, London, Paladin, 1987, pp. 10–11.
3. S. Hynes, *A War Imagined: the First World War and English culture*, London, Pimlico, 1992, p. 447.
4. W. Bakewell, *Hollywood Be Thy Name: random recollections of a movie veteran from silents to TV*, Metuchen, NJ and London, Scarecrow Press, 1991, p. 89.
5. J. Cutts, 'Great Films of the Century: *All Quiet on the Western Front*', *Films and Filming*, vol. 9, April 1963, p. 58.
6. All quotations from the film have been taken from the copy of the screenplay provided by the New York State Archives, Albany, and have been checked against the film.
7. L. Parsons, *Los Angeles Examiner*, 22 April 1930.
8. Unreferenced quotation held in the MPPDA Archives.
9. J. Simmons, 'Film and International Politics: the banning of *All Quiet on the Western Front* in Germany and Austria 1930–1931', *Historian*, vol. 52, 1989, p. 40.
10. *Die Tagebücher von Joseph Goebbels*, Munich, K. G. Saur, 1987, p. 640. I am grateful to Cooper Graham for assistance with this.

1. Cinema, Society and the First World War

1. B. Tuchman, *The Guns of August*, New York, Bantam, 1980, p. 489.
2. S. Hynes, *A War Imagined: the First World War and English culture*, London, Pimlico, 1992, p. x.

3. See P. Barker's *Regeneration*, London, Viking, 1991, *The Eye in the Door*, London, Viking, 1993 and *The Ghost Road*, London, Viking, 1995; S. Faulks, *Birdsong*, London, Hutchinson, 1993 and S. Japrisot, *A Very Long Engagement*, London, Harvill, 1993.

4. This chapter is a summary of my book *Cinema and the Great War*, London, Routledge, 1997. This contains detailed chapters on the following films: *Ned med Vaabnene/Lay Down Your Arms*; *Civilization* and *Intolerance*; *The Big Parade*; *All Quiet on the Western Front*; *Journey's End* and *Tell England*; *Westfront 1918*; *J'accuse* and *La Grande Illusion*; *The Man I Killed*, *The Road Back* and *Three Comrades* and *Paths of Glory*.

5. T. Ramsaye, *A Million and One Nights: a history of the motion picture*, London, Frank Cass, 1964, p. 786.

6. J. Warner quoted in P. A. Soderbergh, '*Aux Armes!*: the rise of the Hollywood war film 1916–1930', *South Atlantic Quarterly*, 65, 1964, p. 514.

7. L. Parsons in *Photoplay*, September 1918, quoted in L. Jacobs, *The Rise of the American Film: a critical history*, New York, Teachers College Press, 1967, pp. 262–3.

8. A. Loos quoted in K. Brownlow, *Hollywood: the pioneers*, London, Collins, 1979, p. 80.

9. Quoted in D. Welch, 'The Proletarian Cinema and the Weimar Republic', *Historical Journal of Film, Radio and Television*, vol. 1, 1981, p. 4.

10. S. Kracauer, *From Caligari to Hitler: a psychological history of the German film*, Princeton, NJ, Princeton University Press, 1947, pp. 66–7.

11. This horrifying book was reissued in the 1980s. See E. Friedrich, *War Against War!* London, The Journeyman Press, 1987.

12. For information on faked scenes in *The Battle of the Somme*, see R. Smither, '"A Wonderful Idea of the Fighting": the question of fakes in *The Battle of the Somme*', *Historical Journal of Film, Radio and Television*, vol. 13, 1993, pp. 149–68.

13. *The Times*, 6 September 1916, quoted in S. Hynes, op. cit., p. 123.

14. *Bioscope*, 10 August 1916, p. xii, quoted in R. Low, *The History of the British Film 1914–1918*, London, Allen and Unwin, 1950, p. 29.

15. House of Commons, *Notices of Motions*, (1927) p. 3403, quoted in Hynes, op. cit., p. 445.

16. Bryher, 'The War from More Angles', *Close Up*, 1, October 1927, p. 45.

17. A. Brunel, *Nice Work*, London, Forbes Robertson, 1949, p. 127.

18. E. Weber, *The Hollow Years: France in the 1930s*, London, Sinclair-Stevenson, 1995, p. 11.

19. A. Gance quoted in K. Brownlow, *The Parade's Gone By*, London, Columbus, 1989, p. 533.

20. A. Gance quoted in ibid., p. 536.

21. M. Balcon, *Michael Balcon Presents … A Lifetime of Films*, London, Hutchinson, 1969, p. 41.

22. R. C. Sherriff, *No Leading Lady: autobiography*, London, Gollancz, 1968, p. 73.

23. R. Graves, *Goodbye to All That*, Harmondsworth, Penguin Books, 1977, p. 54.

24. See E. Cozarinsky, 'G. W. Pabst', in R. Roud (ed.), *Cinema - A Critical Dictionary: the major film-makers*, vol. 2, New York, The Viking Press, p. 759.

25. See E. Johannsen, *Four Infantrymen on the Western Front, 1918*, London, Methuen, 1930.

2. Erich Maria Remarque and *All Quiet on the Western Front*

1. S. Hynes, *A War Imagined: the First World War and English culture*, London, Pimlico, 1992, p. 423.

2. E. Blunden, *Undertones of War*, London, Penguin Books, 1982, p. 7.

3. R. Aldington reviewing H. Read's *In Retreat, Criterion*, vol. 4 (April 1926), quoted in Hynes, op. cit., p. 424.

4. I. Ehrenburg, *Men, Years - Life*, III, London, 1963, pp. 11–12, quoted in M. Eksteins, '*All Quiet on the Western Front* and the Fate of a War', *Journal of Contemporary History*, vol. 15, 1980, p. 346.

5. *Nouvelles littéraires*, 25 October 1930, quoted in Eksteins, '*All Quiet on the Western Front* and the Fate of a War' op. cit., p. 353.

6. J. E., 'Nichts Neues im Westen', *Vossische Zeitung*, 8 November 1928.

7. Figures from *Universal Weekly*, 10 May 1930.

8. See Eksteins, '*All Quiet on the Western Front* and the Fate of a War', op. cit., p. 353.

9. See H. Z. Smith, *Not So Quiet*, London, Virago, 1988.

10. Quoted in '*All Quiet on the Western Front* Souvenir Programme', in M. Kreuger, *Souvenir Programmes of Twelve Classic Movies 1927–1941*, London, Dover, 1977.

11. See the entry for 21 July 1929 in *Die Tagebucher von Joseph Goebbels*, Munich, K. G. Saur, 1987.

12. Information on A. W. Wheen is taken from B. Murdoch, 'Translating the Western Front', *Antiquarian Book Monthly Review*, vol. 28, 1991, pp. 452–60.

13. E. M. Remarque, *All Quiet on the Western Front*, translated by Brian Murdoch, London, Jonathan Cape, 1994. Though this is the definitive version, quotations from the book in this publication are taken from the Wheen translation, as the film was based on this.

14. See *London Mercury*, 21 November 1929, p. 1, quoted in Eksteins, '*All Quiet on the Western Front* and the Fate of a War', op. cit., p. 356.

15. See H. Read, 'A Lost Generation', *Nation and Athenaeum*, vol. 45, 27 April 1929, p. 116, quoted in Hynes, op. cit., p. 440.

16. Quoted in '*All Quiet on the Western Front* Souvenir Programme', op. cit.

17. *Cambridge Review*, 3 May 1929, p. 412.

18. Quoted in '*All Quiet on the Western Front* Souvenir Programme', op. cit.

19. *London Mercury*, 21, 30 January 1930, pp. 194–5, quoted in Eksteins '*All Quiet on the Western Front* and the Fate of a War', op. cit., p. 357.

20. Quoted in E. Weber, *The Hollow Years: France in the 1930s*, London, Sinclair-Stevenson, 1995, p. 18.

21. Quoted in '*All Quiet on the Western Front* Souvenir Programme', op. cit.
22. Ibid.
23. Quoted in advertisement for the book in *Universal Weekly*, 10 May 1930, p. 26.
24. Ibid.
25. Ibid.
26. See 'The End of War? a correspondence between the author of *All Quiet on the Western Front* and General Sir Ian Hamilton, G.C.B, G.C.M.G', *Life and Letters*, vol. 3, November 1929, p. 403.
27. Ibid., p. 405.
28. Ibid., p. 406.
29. *New York Times*, 9 February 1930, quoted in J. Drinkwater, *The Life and Adventures of Carl Laemmle*, London, William Heinemann, 1931, p. 262. Note that other references to these comments have Dr Frick accuse Remarque of 'pacifist *Marxist* propaganda'.
30. *Fränkischer Kurier*, 12 May 1933, cited in H. C. Meyer (ed.), *The Long Generation: Germany from empire to ruin, 1913–1945*, New York, 1973, p. 221, quoted in Eksteins, '*All Quiet on the Western Front* and the Fate of a War', op. cit., p. 363.
31. *Time*, 9 October 1933, quoted in J. Gilbert, *Opposite Attraction: the lives of Erich Maria Remarque and Paulette Goddard*, New York, Pantheon Books, 1995, p. 165.
32. Gilbert, op. cit., p. 166.
33. This section on the life of Erich Maria Remarque has been developed from the work of ibid.; C. R. Barker and R. W. Last, *Erich Maria Remarque*, London, Oswald Woolf, 1979; Eksteins, '*All Quiet on the Western Front* and the Fate of a War', op. cit.; Eksteins, 'War, Memory and Politics: the fate of the film *All Quiet on the Western Front*', *Central European History*, vol. 13, 1980, pp. 60–82.
34. Unattributed quotation in Gilbert, op. cit., p. 14.
35. H.-G. Rabe, quoted in R. A. Firda, *Erich Maria Remarque: a thematic analysis of his novels*, New York, Peter Lang, 1988, p. 21.
36. H. U. Taylor Jr, *Erich Maria Remarque: a literary and film biography*, New York, Peter Lang, 1989, p. 24.
37. E. M. Remarque, quoted in 'Not All Quiet for Remarque', *Literary Digest*, 12 October 1929, p. 19.
38. See S. Weintraub, *A Stillness Heard Round the World: the end of the Great War, November 1918*, Oxford, Oxford University Press, 1987, p. 116.
39. See T. Schneider, quoted in Gilbert, op. cit., pp. 24–5.
40. Remarque, *Literary Digest*, op. cit.
41. C. Riess, quoted in Gilbert, op. cit., p. 88.
42. B. Wilder, quoted in ibid., p. 89.
43. For all the grim details of this appalling episode see Gilbert, ibid., pp. 249–56.
44. See *Det Norske Stortings Nobelkomite: Redegjørelse for Nobels Fredspris 1931*, Oslo, 1931. I am grateful to Patrick Litherland for the translation.
45. Ibid.

46. Remarque quoted in *Motion Picture Herald*, 13 January 1949; cited in Gilbert, op. cit., pp. 121, 123.

3. The 'Boys of *All Quiet*'

1. See the chapter on *All Quiet on the Western Front* in W. Bakewell, *Hollywood Be Thy Name: random recollections of a movie veteran from silents to talkies to TV*, Metuchen, NJ and London, Scarecrow Press, 1991, pp. 70–89.

2. See N. Zierold, *The Moguls: Hollywood's merchants of myth*, Hollywood, Silman-James Press, 1991, p. 118.

3. N. Gabler, *An Empire of Their Own: how the Jews invented Hollywood*, New York, Anchor Books, 1989, p. 47.

4. 'How the Laemmle Exchanges Started', *Film Daily*, 28 February 1926, p. 75, quoted in ibid., p. 52.

5. Carl Laemmle quoted in J. Drinkwater, *The Life and Adventures of Carl Laemmle*, London, William Heinemann, 1931, p. 228.

6. See Drinkwater, op. cit.

7. Ibid., p. 265.

8. H. A. Potamkin, 'The Eyes of the Movie', in L. Jacobs (ed.), *The Compound Cinema: the film writings of Harry Alan Potamkin*, New York and London, Teachers College Press, 1977, p. 255.

9. C. Laemmle, '*All Quiet on the Western Front!*', *Universal Weekly*, 27 July 1929.

10. C. Laemmle, 'The Boy', *Photoplay*, September 1934, p. 38.

11. Lewis Milestone, interview with Kevin Brownlow.

12. L. Milestone quoted in 'Lewis Milestone', in J. Kobal, *People Will Talk*, London, Aurum Press, 1986, p. 149.

13. L. Milestone in P. K. Scheuer, 'Milestone, From Sound to "Mutiny"', *Los Angeles Times*, 22 July 1979.

14. H. Hopper, *Los Angeles Times*, 16 June 1948.

15. Details in this sections have been taken from Lewis Milestone's interview with Kevin Brownlow.

16. Information from the unpublished memoirs of James Bryson held in the British Film Institute Library.

17. N. Zierold, op. cit., p. 111.

18. G. Abbott, *"Mr Abbott"*, New York, Random House, 1963, p. 135.

19. General information on Arthur Edeson has been taken from G. J. Mitchell, 'Making *All Quiet on the Western Front*', *American Cinematographer*, vol. 66, September 1985, p. 39.

20. See Bakewell, op. cit., p. 81.

21. Ibid., p. 2.

22. Letter from Ben Alexander to Jim Sheehan, 1 February 1940.

23. Lewis Milestone interview with Kevin Brownlow.

24. Bakewell, op. cit., p. 87.

25. Information supplied by Kevin Brownlow.

26. *The Times*, 28 December 1957.

27. 'The Filming of *All Quiet* as told by Lewis Milestone to Margaret Chute', *The Pictureyoer*, vol. 20, July 1930, p. 16.

28. Ibid.

29. Lewis Milestone interview with Kevin Brownlow.

30. Ibid.

31. Ibid.

32. L. Ayres quoted in H. G. Luft, 'Lew Ayres', in *Films In Review*, vol. 29, June–July 1978, p. 345.

33. 'Happy to be C. O., Ayres Explains', *New York Times*, 1 April 1942.

34. Lewis Milestone interview with Kevin Brownlow.

35. Hopper quoted in J. L. Yeck, 'An Interview with Lew Ayres', in *Magill's Cinema Annual 1986*, Pasadena, Salem Press, 1986, p. 18.

36. Ibid.

37. Luft, op. cit., p. 351.

38. F. Zinnemann, *Fred Zinnemann: an autobiography*, London, Bloomsbury, 1992, p. 23.

39. R. Parrish, *Growing Up in Hollywood*, New York, Harcourt Brace Jovanovich, 1976, p. 72.

40. Ayres quoted in P. McGilligan, *George Cukor: a double life*, London, Faber and Faber, 1991, p. 65.

41. Ibid, p. 66.

42. Bakewell, op. cit., p. 74.

43. See G. Lambert, *On Cukor*, New York, Putnams, 1972, p. 25.

4. The Troubled Production

1. Harold Goodwin interview with Kevin Brownlow.

2. S. Hynes, *A War Imagined: the First World War and English culture*, London, Pimlico, 1992, p. 448.

3. See H. Cobb, *Paths of Glory*, New York, Viking, 1935, p. 75.

4. Lewis Milestone interview with Kevin Brownlow.

5. See 'Personally Conducted Visit to "All Quiet on the Western Front" Battlefield with Ivan St. Johns', *Universal Weekly*, 8 February 1930.

6. R. Leighton, quoted in V. Brittain, *War Diary 1913–1917*, cited in Hynes, op. cit., p. 112. For further details see P. Berry and M. Bostridge, *Vera Brittain: a life*, London, Chatto and Windus, 1995.

7. *Universal Weekly*, 23 November 1929. The story of the names in the uniforms may be only partly true!

8. See 'War Nurses Visit Movie Battlefields of "All Quiet" Film', *Universal Weekly*, 8 March 1930.

9. A. Edeson quoted in G. J. Mitchell, 'Making *All Quiet on the Western Front*', in *American Cinematographer*, vol. 66, September 1985, p. 39.

10. The full text of the Abbott version is contained in S. Thomas, *Great*

American Screenplays, New York, Crown, 1986, pp. 13–72. This is the baseline screenplay for this comparison.

11. E. M. Remarque, *All Quiet on the Western Front*, London, Mayflower-Dell, 1963, p. 192.

12. Quoted in Thomas, op. cit., p. 72.

13. L. Milestone, quoted in L. Tajiri, 'Long Search for an Ending', *The Denver Post*, 10 September 1964.

14. L. Milestone, quoted in K. Brownlow, *The War, the West and the Wilderness*, London, Secker and Warburg, 1979, p. 217.

15. L. Milestone, quoted in Tajiri, op. cit.

16. Lewis Milestone interview with Kevin Brownlow.

17. See Milestone's comments in D. Diehl, 'Directors Go to Their Movies: Lewis Milestone', in *Action*, vol. 7, July/August 1972, p. 11.

18. 'The Filming of *All Quiet* as told by Lewis Milestone to Margaret Chute', in *The Picturegoer*, vol. 20, July 1930, p. 15.

19. Lewis Milestone interview with Kevin Brownlow.

20. Ibid.

21. Ibid.

22. Report of what Milestone said Anderson said, in 'The Filming of *All Quiet* as told by Lewis Milestone to Margaret Chute', op. cit.

23. F. Kohner, *The Magician of Sunset Boulevard: the improbable life of Paul Kohner, Hollywood agent*, Palos Verdes, Morgan Press, 1977, p. 50.

24. See 'Louis Wolheim to Play Big Role in "All Quiet"', in *Universal Weekly*, 7 December 1929, p. 1.

25. F. Zinnemann, *Fred Zinnemann: an autobiography*, London, Bloomsbury, 1992, p. 23.

26. See Bakewell, op. cit., pp. 85–6.

5. Reception, Condemnation and Censorship

1. L. K. Dean, '*All Quiet on the Western Front*: the greatest human document of the war comes to the screen', *American Cinematographer*, March 1930, p. 11.

2. *Variety*, 7 May 1930.

3. *Los Angeles Examiner*, 22 April 1930.

4. *Los Angeles Evening Herald*, 22 April 1930.

5. G. Rogers, *Ginger: my story*, London, Headline, 1991, p. 61.

6. Ibid., p. 62.

7. *New York Times*, 30 April 1930.

8. H. Barnes in *Herald Tribune*, quoted in 'War Without Glamour on the Film', in *Literary Digest*, 105, 17 May 1930, p. 20.

9. *The Nation*, 11 June 1930.

10. *Photoplay*, June 1930, p. 57.

11. H. A. Potamkin, in L. Jacobs (ed.), *The Compound Cinema: the film writings of Harry Alan Potamkin*, New York and London, Teachers College Press, 1977, p. xxxvi.

12. T. Delehunty quoted in 'War Without Glamour on the Film', op. cit.
13. Quoted in M. Riva, *Marlene Dietrich*, London, Bloomsbury, 1993, p. 86.
14. H. Hughes to Lewis Milestone, 15 July 1930.
15. Details of American censorship are taken from MPPDA files in the Margaret Herrick Library, Academy of Motion Picture Arts and Sciences in Los Angeles.
16. Letter from Jason Joy to Carl Laemmle Jr, 21 August 1929, in ibid.
17. Report of première of *All Quiet on the Western Front* by J. B. M. Fisher, 29 April 1930.
18. Quoted in M. Seton, *Sergei M. Eisenstein: a biography*, London, Dobson Books, 1978, p. 168.
19. Ibid., p. 156.
20. See S. Eisenstein, *Immoral Memories: an autobiography*, London, Peter Owen, 1985, p. 183.
21. Telegram from Frank Pease to various politicians and others, *Hollywood United Technical Directors Association*, 28 April 1930.
22. Ibid.
23. Letter from R. H. Cochrane to Colonel Wingate, MPPDA, 12 May 1930.
24. Undated letter from Boy Scouts Association of America, MPPDA.
25. *The Nation*, 2 July 1930, p. 7.
26. *Photoplay*, December 1931, pp. 57, 113.
27. Details for this section are taken from the letter and accompanying documentation from Anne Jones, Chair, Ontario Film Board (undated, but 1987) replying to Jim Sheehan.
28. Memorandum dated 17 July 1930, found in the office of the New Zealand Chief Censor of Film.
29. L. George in *News Chronicle*, quoted in *Film-Revy*, 2, March 1931, p. 28.
30. S. W. Carroll, in the *Sunday Times*, 22 June 1930, quoted in M. Eksteins, 'War, Memory and Politics: the fate of the film *All Quiet on the Western Front*', in *Central European History*, vol. 13, 1980, p. 62.
31. J. Agate, 'All Quiet on the Western Front', 25 June 1930, in *Around Cinemas*, Home and Van Thal, 1946, p. 69.
32. *Reynolds News*, 8 June 1930.
33. *The Times*, 6 June 1930.
34. *Kinematograph Weekly*, 12 June 1930.
35. *Bioscope*, 11 June 1930.
36. See C. A. Lejeune, *Cinema*, London, Alexander Maclehose and Co., 1931, p. 221.
37. P. Rotha, *Celluloid: the film to-day*, London, Longmans, Green, 1933, p. 133–4.
38. Details for this section have been taken from the letter and accompanying documentation from A. W. Everard, Chief Censor of Films, Auckland (19 August 1987), replying to Jim Sheehan.
39. Ibid.
40. Ibid.

41. Ibid.

42. From advertisement for film in *New Zealand Herald*, 7 August 1930.

43. Memorandum from Joseph Breen, 16 November 1939, MPPDA.

44. Details for this section have been taken from the letter and accompanying documentation from David Haines, Acting Chief Censor, Attorney General's Office, Sydney (10 June 1987), replying to Jim Sheehan.

45. From advertisement for the film in *Everyones*, 25 June 1930, p. 14.

46. Various sources have been used for this section. These include MPPDA files; Eksteins, 'War, Memory and Politics ... ', op. cit.; J. Simmons, 'Film and International Politics: the banning of *All Quiet on the Western Front* in Germany and Austria 1930–1931', in *Historian*, vol. 52, 1989; and *Tormented Celluloid: the fate of the cinema classic 'All Quiet on the Western Front'*, ZDF, directed by Hans Beller, 25 November 1984.

47. 'Mr Laemmle Returns', *New York Times*, 6 October 1929.

48. Joy's note in MPPDA files dated 15 February 1930. Joy felt that Von Hentig was amenable as he wanted a role as a special adviser to Hollywood on problems relating to German distribution, as Valentin Mandelstamm was conducting for the French government – see later (Joy memorandum, 7 April 1930).

49. *Der Angriff*, 6 December 1930, quoted in Simmons, op. cit., p. 46.

50. Memorandum to Hays, 6 December 1930, MPPDA.

51. See L. Riefenstahl, *The Sieve of Time*, London, Quartet, 1992, pp. 65–6.

52. All quotations taken from '*All Quiet* Banned by Reich Censors', *New York Times*, 12 December 1930.

53. *Der Angriff*, 12 December 1930, quoted in Simmons, op. cit., p. 51.

54. Quoted in the Danish newspaper *Aftenposten*, 13 December 1930.

55. Sackett to Secretary of State, 17 December 1930, *Foreign Relations*, 1931, quoted in Simmons, op. cit., pp. 51–2.

56. Quoted in the Danish newspaper *Aftenposten*, 13 December 1930.

57. *Manchester Guardian*, 12 December 1930.

58. For details of Spiegel's role in *All Quiet on the Western Front*, see Simmons, op. cit. See also A. Sinclair, *Spiegel – the man behind the pictures*, London, Weidenfeld and Nicholson, 1987 (although this is not a good biography).

59. Undated report in MPPDA files. Emphasis in original.

60. Ayres quoted in '*Tormented Celluloid*, op. cit.

61. Mandelstamm to Joy, 2 April 1930, MPPDA.

62. *Film Daily*, 2 November 1930.

63. *Variety*, 24 December 1930.

64. J. Bernier, *Ciné-Miroir*, 17 October 1930, p. 659.

65. *Dagbladet*, 16 March 1931.

66. *Dagbladet*, 18 March 1931.

67. *Nationen*, 16 March 1931.

68. *Morgenbladet*, 16 March 1931.

69. See Sinclair, op. cit., p. 18.

70. Ibid.

6. The Aftermath: *The Road Back, Three Comrades* and *All Quiet on the Western Front* (1932–1997)

1. W. Owen quoted in mini-biography in B. Gardner, *Up the Line to Death: the war poets 1914–1918*, London, Methuen, 1976, p. 176.

2. E. M. Remarque, *All Quiet on the Western Front*, London, Mayflower-Dell, 1963, p. 190.

3. See entry on film in D. Shipman, *The Story of Cinema*, vol. 1, London, Hodder and Stoughton, 1982, pp. 274–5.

4. From *All Quiet on the Western Front: Universal's continuity and dialogue, revised version as of March 1st 1934.*

5. 'Big Money For You', *Universal Weekly*, 3 March 1934.

6. Ibid.

7. Harry Zehner, Universal, to Joseph Breen, 13 October 1936, MPPDA.

8. George Gyssling to Joseph Breen, 30 September 1936, MPPDA.

9. Joseph Breen to Harry Zehner, 14 October 1936, MPPDA.

10. George Gyssling to Larry Blake, 9 April 1937, quoted in J. Curtis, *James Whale*, London, Faber and Faber, 1998.

11. Both quotes by Michael Blake, talking about his father to James Curtis. Quoted in Curtis, op. cit.

12. John Emery quoted in *Motion Picture Herald*, 19 June 1937.

13. *Life*, June 1937.

14. *Variety*, 8 June 1937.

15. *Cue*, 19 June 1937, p. 34.

16. L. Parsons, quoted in Universal publicity in *Motion Picture Daily*, 25 June 1937.

17. *Hollywood Spectator*, 3 July 1937.

18. *New York Times*, 16 June 1937, p. 25.

19. Ibid.

20. J. Russell Taylor (ed.), *The Pleasure Dome: Graham Greene - the collected film criticism 1935–1940*, Oxford, Oxford University Press, 1980, pp. 172–3.

21. *Film Weekly*, 9 October 1937, p. 32.

22. *Monthly Film Bulletin*, 31 August 1937, p. 175.

23. *Time*, 28 June 1937.

24. *New Masses*, undated news cutting in MPPDA.

25. The criticism was justified: a terrible screenplay from, ironically, a writer about to embark on what could have been his greatest book, *The Last Tycoon*. See M. Bruccoli, *F. Scott Fitzgerald's Screenplay for Three Comrades by Erich Maria Remarque*, Carbondale and Edwardsville, Southern Illinois University Press, 1978.

26. Quoted in K. Geist, *Pictures Will Talk: the life and times of Joseph L. Mankiewicz*, New York, Da Capo Press, 1978, p. 91.

27. E. M. Remarque, *Three Comrades*, London, The Book Club, 1938, p. 58.

28. *New York Times*, 3 June 1938, p. 17.

29. *Newsweek*, 6 June 1938, p. 23.

30. *Variety*, 25 May 1938, p. 12.
31. From *Universal's Continuity and Dialogue, Revised Version as of September 18th 1939*.
32. *Commonweal*, 13 October 1939, p. 564.
33. *Newsweek*, 9 October 1939, p. 36.
34. *Time*, 2 October 1939, p. 49.
35. *New York Times*, 9 October 1939.
36. Lewis Milestone to Jim Sheehan, 6 April 1964.
37. See *Tormented Celluloid: the fate of the cinema classic 'All Quiet on the Western Front'*, ZDF, directed by Hans Beller, 25 November 1984.
38. New York *Herald Tribune*, 30 July 1950.
39. Ibid.
40. See 'U.S. Lists Movies it Limits Abroad', *New York Times*, 24 May 1959.
41. See letter from R. Mitchell in *American Cinematographer*, 2, 1986.
42. N. Andrews, *Financial Times*, 6 June 1980.
43. D. Robinson, *The Times*, 6 June 1980.
44. Information supplied by Jurgen Labenski. See also J. Kindred, 'ZDF TV Skeds "Western Front" in Labenski Style', *Variety*, 4 April 1984, p. 47.
45. Lewis Milestone to Jim Sheehan, op. cit.

7. The Greatness and Continuing Significance of *All Quiet on the Western Front*

1. J. L. Yeck, 'An Interview with Lew Ayres', *Magill's Cinema Annual 1986*, Pasadena, Salem Press, 1986, p. 13.
2. C. Laemmle quoted in *Exhibitors' World Herald*, 13 December 1930, p. 25, and cited in J. Simmons, 'Film and International Politics: the banning of *All Quiet on the Western Front* in Germany and Austria 1930–1931', in *Historian*, vol. 52, 1989, p. 47.
3. See J. Baxter, *Stanley Kubrick: a biography*, London, HarperCollins, 1997.
4. See H. Barnes in *Herald Tribune*, quoted in 'War Without Glamour on the Film', in *Literary Digest*, 105, 17 May 1930, p. 20.
5. D. W. Griffith, *Los Angeles Evening Herald*, 3 June 1930.
6. D. Robinson in A. Lloyd (ed.), *Movies of the Thirties*, London, Orbis Books, 1985.
7. Anonymous reviewer in 'War Without Glamour on the Film', op. cit.
8. See Renoir's comments in R. Hughes, *Film: Book 2 – Films of Peace and War*, New York, Grove Press, 1962, p. 183: 'In 1936 I made a picture named *La Grande Illusion* in which I tried to express all my deep feelings for the cause of peace. This film was very successful. Three years later the war broke out. That is the only answer I can find to your very interesting enquiry.'

Postscript

1. All dates given for these publications are for the first English publication.

2. For details of this strange episode see J. Gilbert, *Opposite Attraction: the lives of Erich Maria Remarque and Paulette Goddard*, New York: Pantheon Books, 1995, p. 456.

3. For further details see *Important Printed and Manuscript Music and Continental Manuscripts*, London: Sotheby's, 1 December 1995 and Garner, C., 'Epic manuscript sold for £276,000', *Independent*, 2 December 1995.

Select Bibliography

This bibliography contains most of the material used in the preparation of this book. It therefore includes information on books and articles not listed in the notes. The dates of publication are those of editions used in this book. They are not necessarily the date of first publication.

Unpublished Documents

BFI microfiches, British Film Institute Library, London.

Censor office files in New Zealand, France, Germany, New Zealand and Australia.

FBI Files on Lewis Milestone, Washington, DC.

Interviews with those involved in the film by Kevin Brownlow and Andrew Kelly.

Lewis Milestone papers, Margaret Herrick Library, Academy of Motion Picture Arts and Sciences, Los Angeles.

MPPDA (Motion Picture Producers and Distributors of America) files, Margaret Herrick Library, Academy of Motion Picture Arts and Sciences, Los Angeles.

Screenplays held in the New York State Archives, Albany, New York.

Journals, Newspapers and Annual Publications

Action; Aftenposten; American Cinematographer; American Film; Berliner Tageblatt; Bioscope; Cambridge Review; Ciné-Miroir; Close Up; Commonweal; Critique Cinématographique; Cue; Dagbladet; Daily Express; The Denver Post; Der Angriff; Evening News; Everyones (Australia); *Exhibitors' World Herald; Film and History; Film Comment; Film Daily; Film Quarterly; Film Revy; Film Weekly; Film-Kurier; Films and Filming; Films in Review;*

Select Bibliography 191

Financial Times; Focus on Film; Folkets avis; Frankfurter Zeitung; Fränkischer Kurier; Guardian; Historian; Historical Journal of Film, Radio and Television; The Hollywood Reporter; Hollywood Spectator; Journal of Central European Affairs; Journal of Contemporary History; Kinematograph Weekly; Krieg und Literatur; Life and Letters; Life Magazine; London Mercury; Die Literarische Welt; Literary Digest; Los Angeles Examiner; Los Angeles Evening Herald; Los Angeles Times; Magill's Cinema Annual; Monthly Film Bulletin; Morganbladet; Motion Picture Daily; Motion Picture Herald; Motion Picture Magazine; Motion Picture News; Motion Picture Review; Motion Picture World; Moving Picture World; The Nation; Nation and Athenaeum; Nationaltidende; Nationen; New Masses; Nouvelles littéraires; Herald Tribune; New York Times; New Yorker; New Zealand Herald; Newsweek; Photoplay; Picturegoer; Politiken; Quarterly Review of Film Studies; Reynolds News; Socialdemokraten; The South Atlantic Quarterly; Spectator; Sunday Times; Time; The Times; Universal Weekly; Variety; Vossische Zeitung

Other Published Documents

Abbott, G., *'Mr Abbott!'*, New York, Random House, 1963.

Agate, J., *Around Cinemas*, Home and Van Thal, 1946.

Agel, J. (ed.), *The Making of Kubrick's 2001*, New York, Signet, 1970.

Armes, R., *A Critical History of British Cinema*, London, Secker & Warburg, 1978.

— *French Cinema*, New York, Oxford University Press, 1985.

Atwell, L., *G. W. Pabst*, Boston, Twayne, 1977.

Bakewell, W., *Hollywood Be Thy Name: random recollections of a movie veteran from silents to talkies to TV*, Metuchen, N. J. and London, Scarecrow Press, 1991.

Balcon, M., *Michael Balcon Presents ... A Lifetime of Films*, London, Hutchinson, 1969.

Barker, C. R. and R. W. Last, *Erich Maria Remarque*, London, Oswald Woolf, 1979.

Barker, P., *Regeneration*, London, Viking, 1991.

— *The Eye in the Door*, London, Viking, 1993.

— *The Ghost Road*, London, Viking, 1995.

Baxter, J., *King Vidor*, New York, 1976.

— *Stanley Kubrick*, London, HarperCollins, 1997.

Bazin, A., *Jean Renoir*, New York, Simon and Schuster, 1986.

Bergman, A., *We're in the Money: depression America and its films*, Chicago, Elephant Paperbacks, 1992.

Bergonzi, B., *Heroes' Twilight: a study of the literature of the great war*, London, Macmillan, revised edition, 1980.

Berry, P. and M. Bostridge, *Vera Brittain: a life*, London, Chatto and Windus, 1995.

Black, G. D., *Hollywood Censored: morality codes, Catholics, and the movies*, Cambridge, Cambridge University Press, 1994.

Blunden, E., *Undertones of War*, London, Penguin, 1982.

Bordwell, D., *The Films of Carl-Theodor Dreyer*, Berkeley, University of California Press, 1981.

Braudy, L., *Jean Renoir: the world of his films*, London, Robson, 1977.

Brock, P., *Twentieth-Century Pacifism*, New York, Van Nostrand Reinhold, 1970.

Brogan, H., *Longman History of the United States of America*, London, Longman, 1985.

Brownlow, K., *Hollywood: the pioneers*, London, Collins, 1979.

— *The War, the West and the Wilderness*, London, Secker & Warburg, 1979.

— *Napoleon: Abel Gance's classic film*, London, Cape, 1983.

— *The Parade's Gone By*, London, Columbus, 1989.

Bruccoli, M. (ed.), *Three Comrades*, Carbondale and Edwardsville, Southern Illinois University Press, 1978.

Butler, I., *Silent Magic: rediscovering the silent film era*, London, Columbus Books, 1987.

Brunel, A., *Nice Work*, London, Forbes Robertson, 1949.

Campbell, C. W., *Reel America and World War I*, Jefferson, NC and London, McFarland, 1985.

Caute, D., *Joseph Losey: a revenge on life*, London, Faber and Faber, 1994.

Ceplair, L. and S. Englund, *The Inquisition in Hollywood: politics in the film community, 1930–1960*.

Ciment, M., *Conversations With Losey*, London and New York, Methuen, 1985.

Cobb, H., *Paths of Glory*, New York, Viking, 1935.

O'Connor, J. E. and M. A. Jackson (eds), *American History/American Film: interpreting the Hollywood image*, New York, Frederick Ungar Publishing Company, 1979.

O'Connor, J. E. (ed. and intro.), *I Am a Fugitive from a Chain Gang*, Wisconsin, London, University of Wisconsin Press, 1981.

Curtis, J., *James Whale*, London, Faber and Faber, 1998.

O'Dell, P., *Griffith and the Rise of Hollywood*, London, Zwemmer, 1970.

Dibbets, K. and B. Hogenkamp (eds), *Film and the First World War*, Amsterdam, Amsterdam University Press, 1995.

Dixon, N. F., *On the Psychology of Military Incompetence*, London, Futura, 1979.

Douglas, K., *The Ragman's Son*, London, Simon and Schuster, 1988.

Dowd, N. and D. Shepard, *King Vidor: a Director's Guild of America oral history project*, New Jersey and London, Director's Guild of America and Scarecrow Press.

Drew, W., *D. W. Griffith's* Intolerance: *its genesis and its vision*, Jefferson, NC and London, McFarland, 1986.

Drinkwater, J., *The Life and Adventures of Carl Laemmle*, London, William Heinemann, 1931.

Durgnat, R., *Jean Renoir*, Berkeley and Los Angeles, University of California Press, 1974.

Durgnat, R. and S. Simmon, *King Vidor, American*, Berkeley and London, University of California Press, 1988.

Eisenstein, S., *Immoral memories: an autobiography*, London, Peter Owen, 1985.

Eisner, L. H., *The Haunted Screen: Expressionism in the German cinema and the influence of Max Reinhardt*, London, Secker & Warburg, 1973.

Engberg, M., *Dansk Stumfilm – de store ar*, Copenhagen, Rhodos, 1977.

Faulks, S., *Birdsong*, London, Hutchinson, 1993.

Firda, R. A., *Erich Maria Remarque: a thematic analysis of his novels*, New York, Peter Lang, 1988.

Frayling, C., *Things to Come*, London, British Film Institute, 1995.

Friedrich, E., *War Against War!*, London, Journeyman Press, 1987.

Fussell, P., *The Great War and Modern Memory*, Oxford, Oxford University Press, 1977.

Gabler, N., *An Empire of Their Own: how the Jews invented Hollywood*, New York and London, Anchor Books, 1989.

Gance, A., *Prisme*, Paris, Gallimard, 1930.

Gay, P., *Weimar Culture: the outsider as insider*, London, Penguin, 1992.

Gardner, B., *Up the Line to Death: the war poets 1914-1918*, London, Methuen, 1976.

Geist, K., *Pictures Will Talk: the life and films of Joseph L. Mankiewicz*, New York, Da Capo Press, 1978.

Gilbert, J., *Opposite Attraction: the lives of Erich Maria Remarque and Paulette Goddard*, New York, Pantheon Books, 1995.

Gilbert, M., *First World War*, London, HarperCollins, 1995.

Gill, A., *A Dance Between Flames: Berlin between the wars*, London, Abacus, 1995.

Gish, L., *The Movies, Mr Griffith and Me*, London, Columbus Books, 1988.

Glover, J. and J. Silkin (ed. and intro.), *The Penguin Book of First World War Prose*, London, Viking, 1989.

Goebbels, J., *Die Tagebücher von Joseph Goebbels*, Munich, K. G. Saur, 1987.

Graves, R., *Goodbye to All That*, Harmondsworth, Penguin, 1977.

Hamman, B., *Bertha von Suttner: ein leben für den frieden*, Munich, Zurich, Piper, 1986.

Hampton, B. B., *History of the American Film Industry: from its beginnings to 1931*, New York, Dover, 1970.

Hardy, F. (ed. and comp.), *Grierson on Documentary*, London, Faber and Faber, 1966.

Harth, D., D. Schubert and R. M. Schmidt (eds), *Pazifismus: zwischen den Weltkriegen*, Heidelberg, HVA, 1985.

Herbert, A. P., *The Secret Battle*, Oxford, Oxford University Press, 1982.

Hibberd, D. (ed. and intro.), *Wilfred Owen: war poems and others*, London, Chatto and Windus, 1976.

Hove, A. (ed. and intro.), *Gold Diggers of 1933*, Wisconsin and London, University of Wisconsin Press, 1980.

Hughes, R. (ed.), *Film: Book 2 – Films of Peace and War*, New York, Grove Press, 1962.

Hynes, S., *A War Imagined: the First World War and English Culture*, London, Pimlico, 1990.

Isenberg, M. T., *War on Film: the American cinema and World War I, 1914–1941*, London and Toronto, Associated University Presses, 1981.

Jacobs, L. (ed.), *The Compound Cinema: the film writings of Harry Alan Potamkin*, New York and London, Teachers College Press, 1977.

— *The Rise of the American Film: a critical history*, New York, Teachers College Press, 1967.

Japrisot, S., *A Very Long Engagement*, London, Harvill, 1993.

Johannsen, E., *Four Infantrymen on the Western Front, 1918*, London, Methuen, 1930.

Jowett, G., *Film – The Democratic Art: a social history of American film*, London, Focal Press, 1976.

Kelly, A., *Cinema and the Great War*, London, Routledge, 1997.

Kempf, B., *Suffragette for Peace: the life of Bertha von Suttner*, London, Oswald Wolff, 1972.

Kohner, F., *The Magician of Sunset Boulevard: the improbable life of Paul Kohner, Hollywood Agent*, Palos Verdes, Morgan Press, 1977.

Kracauer, S., *From Caligari to Hitler: a psychological history of the German film*, New Jersey, Princeton University Press, 1947.

Kreuger, M. (ed.), *Souvenir Programmes of Twelve Classic Movies 1927-1941*, New York, Dover, 1977.

Lambert, G., *On Cukor*, New York, Putnams, 1972.

Leff, L. J. and J. L. Simmons, *The Dame in the Kimono: Hollywood, censorship and the Production Code from the 1920s to the 1960s*, London, Grove Weidenfeld, 1990.

Lejeune, C. A., *Cinema*, London, Alexander Maclehose, 1931.

Low, R., *The History of the British Film 1914–1918*, London, George Allen and Unwin, 1950.

— *The History of the British Film 1918–1929*, London, George Allen and Unwin, 1971.

— *The History of the British Film 1929–1939: films of comment and persuasion of the 1930s*, London, George Allen and Unwin, 1979.

Lyon, C. (ed.), *The International Dictionary of Films and Filmmakers, vol. II: directors/filmmakers*, London, Macmillan, 1984.

McGilligan, P., *George Cukor: a double life*. London, Faber and Faber, 1991.

Magill, F. N. (ed.), *Magill's Survey of Cinema*, Englewood Cliffs, NJ, Salem, 1985.

Maria Remarque, E., *Three Comrades*, London, Book Club, 1938.

— *All Quiet on the Western Front*, London, Mayflower-Dell, 1963.

— *The Road Back*, London, Mayflower, 1979.

— *All Quiet on the Western Front* (trans. B. Murdoch), London, Jonathan Cape, 1994.

Masterworks of the French Cinema, London, Faber and Faber, 1988.

May, L., *Screening out the Past: the birth of mass culture and the motion picture industry*, Chicago and London, University of Chicago Press, 1983.

Minney, R. J., *Puffin Asquith: the biography of the Honourable Anthony Asquith, aristocrat, aesthete, prime minister's son and brilliant film maker*, London, Leslie Frewin, 1973.

Mock, J. R., *Censorship 1917*, New York, Da Capo Press, revised edition, 1972.

Monaco, P., *Cinema and Society: France and Germany during the twenties*, New York and Oxford, Elsevier, 1976.

Murdoch, B., *Fighting Songs and Warring Words: popular lyrics of two world wars*, London, Routledge, 1990.

Parrish, R., *Growing Up in Hollywood*. New York, Harcourt Brace Jovanovich, 1976.

Pearson, G., *Flashback: an autobiography of a British film maker*, London, George Allen and Unwin, 1957.

Percy, W., *The Moviegoer*, London, Paladin, 1987.

Pierson, R. R. (ed.), *Women and Peace: theoretical, historical and practical perspectives*, London, Croom Helm, 1989.

Poirier, L., *Vingt-quatre images a la seconde*, Paris, Mame, 1953.

Ramsaye, T., *A Million and One Nights: a history of the motion picture*, London, Frank Cass, 1964.

Reeves, N., *Official British Film Propaganda During The First World War*, Beckenham, Croom Helm, 1986.

Renoir, J., *My Life and My Films*, London, Collins, 1974.

Rentschler, E. (ed.), *The Films of G. W. Pabst: an extraterritorial cinema*, New Brunswick and London, Rutgers University Press, 1990.

Richards, J., *Visions of Yesterday*, London, Routledge, 1973.

— *The Age of the Dream Palace: cinema and society in Britain 1930–1939*, London, Routledge, 1984.

— *Happiest Days: the public schools in English fiction*, Manchester, Manchester University Press, 1988.

Riefenstahl, L., *The Sieve of Time*, London, Quartet, 1992.

Riva, M., *Marlene Dietrich*, London, Bloomsbury, 1992.

The Road to Glory: a screenplay, Carbondale and Edwardsville, Southern Illinois University Press, 1981.

Robertson, J. C., *The British Board of Film Censors: film censorship in Britain, 1896–1950*, Beckenham, Croom Helm, 1985.

— *The Hidden Cinema: British film censorship in action, 1913–1972*, London, Routledge, 1989.

Roddick, N., *A New Deal in Entertainment: Warner Brothers in the 1930s*, London, British Film Institute, 1983.

Rogers, G., *Ginger: my story*, London, Headline, 1991.

Rotha, P., *Celluloid: the film to-day*, London, Longmans, Green and Co., 1933.

— (with R. Griffith), *The Film Till Now: a survey of world cinema*, London, Spring Books, 1967.

Roud, R. (ed.), *Cinema – A Critical Dictionary: the major film-makers, vol. 2*, New York, Viking Press, 1980.

Russell Taylor, J. (ed.), *The Pleasure Dome: Graham Greene – the collected film criticism 1935–1940*, Oxford, Oxford University Press, 1980.

Sassoon, S., *Memoirs of an Infantry Officer*, London, Faber and Faber, 1978.

— *The War Poems*, London, Faber and Faber, 1983.

Schatz, T., *The Genius of the System: Hollywood filmmaking in the studio era*, London, Simon and Schuster, 1989.

Schickel, R., *D. W. Griffith*, London, Pavilion, 1984.

Sesonske, A., *Jean Renoir: the French films 1924–1939*, Cambridge, MA and London, Harvard University Press, 1980.

Seton, M., *Sergei M. Eisenstein – A Biography*, London, Dennis Dobson, 1978.

Sherriff, R. C. and V. Bartlett, *Journey's End: a novel*, London, Gollancz, 1930.

Sherriff, R. C., *No Leading Lady: autobiography*, London, Gollancz, 1968.

Shipman, D., *The Story of Cinema: vol. 1*, London, Hodder and Stoughton, 1982.

Silkin, J., *Out of Battle: the poetry of the great war*, London and New York, Ark, 1987.

Sinclair, A., *Spiegel – the man behind the pictures*, London, Weidenfeld and Nicholson, 1987.

Sklar, R., *Movie-Made America: a cultural history of American movies*, London, Elm Tree/Chappell and Company, 1978.

Slide, A., *The Picture Dancing on the Screen: poetry of the cinema*, New York, Vestal Press, nd.

— (ed.), *Robert Goldstein and The Spirit of '76*, New Jersey and London, Scarecrow Press, 1993.

— *Early American Cinema*, New Jersey and London, Scarecrow Press, revised edition, 1994.

Smith, H., *Not So Quiet*, London, Virago, 1988.

Sorlin, P., *The Film in History: restaging the past*, Oxford, Basil Blackwell, 1980.

— *European Cinemas, European Societies 1939–1990*, London, Routledge, 1991.

Spears, J., *Hollywood: the golden era*, New York, Castle Books, 1971.

Stallworthy, J., *Wilfred Owen*, Oxford, Oxford University Press, 1988.

Suttner, B., *Lay Down Your Arms: the autobiography of Martha von Tilling*, London, Longmans, Green and Co., 1894.

Taylor, A. J. P., *English History 1914–1945*, Oxford, Oxford University Press, 1965.

Taylor, H. U. Jr, *Erich Maria Remarque: a literary and film biography*, New York, Peter Lang, 1989.

Taylor, P. M., *Munitions of the Mind: war propaganda from the ancient world to the nuclear age*, Wellingborough, Patrick Stephens, 1990.

Thomas, S. (ed.), *Best American Screenplays: first series*, New York, Crown, 1986.

Trumbo, D., *Johnny Got His Gun*, London, Touchstone, 1994.

Tuchman, B. W., *The Guns of August*, New York, Bantam, 1976.

Vidor, K., *A Tree is a Tree*, London and New York, Longmans, Green and Co., 1954.

Wagenknecht, E., *The Movies in the Age of Innocence*, Norman, University of Oklahoma Press, 1962.

Walker, A., *Stanley Kubrick Directs*, London, Abacus, 1973.

Walker, J. (ed.), *Halliwell's Film Guide*, London, Grafton, revised edition, 1992.

— *Halliwell's Filmgoer's Companion*, London, HarperCollins, 1993.

Warren, L. (ed.), *How I Filmed the War by G. H. Malins OBE*, London, 1920.

Weber, E., *The Hollow Years: France in the 1930s*, London, Sinclair-Stevenson, 1995.

Weinberg, H., *The Lubitsch Touch: a critical study*, New York, Dover, 1977.

Weintraub, S., *A Stillness Heard Round the World: the end of the Great War November 1918*, Oxford, Oxford University Press, 1985.

Williamson, H., *The Patriot's Progress*, London, Cardinal, 1991.

Wollenberg, H. H., *Fifty Years of German Films*, London, Falcon Press, 1948.

Wright, B., *The Long View: a personal perspective on world cinema*, London, Secker & Warburg, 1974.

Zierold, N., *The Moguls: Hollywood's merchants of myth*, Hollywood, Silman-James Press, 1991.

Zinnemann, F., *Fred Zinnemann: an autobiography*, London, Bloomsbury, 1992.

Articles

Abrams, I., 'Bertha von Suttner and the Nobel Peace Prize', *Journal of Central European Affairs*, October 1962, vol. 27, pp. 286–307.

Badsey, S. D., 'Battle of the Somme: British war-propaganda', *Historical Journal of Film, Radio and Television*, 1983, vol. 3, pp. 99–115.

Bier, J., 'Cobb and Kubrick: author and auteur (*Paths of Glory* as novel and film)', *The Virginia Quarterly Review*, Summer 1985, pp. 453–71.

Borger, L., 'Les Croix de bois de Raymond Bernard', *Cinématographe*, July–August 1983, pp. 31–5.

Burgess, J., 'The "Anti-Militarism" of Stanley Kubrick', *Film Quarterly*, 1964, vol. 18, pp. 4–11.

Cutts, J., 'Great Films of the Century: *All Quiet on the Western Front*', *Films and Filming*, April 1963, vol. 9, pp. 55–8.

Diehl, D., 'Directors go to Their Movies: Jean Renoir', *Action*, May–June 1972, vol. 7, pp. 2–5, 8.

Eksteins, M., 'War, Memory, and Politics: the fate of the film *All Quiet on the Western Front*', *Central European History*, 1980, vol. 13, pp. 60–82.

Everson, W. K., 'Rediscovery', *Films in Review*, March 1985, pp. 172–5.

Finler, J., 'Grand Illusion', in *Masterworks of the French Cinema*, London, Faber and Faber, 1988, pp. 335–41.

Greenberg, J., 'War, Wheat & Steel: King Vidor interviewed by Joel Greenberg', *Sight and Sound*, 1968, vol. 37, pp. 192–7.

Isenberg, M. T., 'An Ambiguous Pacifism: a retrospective on World War I films, 1930–1938', *Journal of Popular Film*, 1975, vol. iv, pp. 98–115.

— 'The Mirror of Democracy: reflections of the war films of World War I, 1917–1919', *Journal of Popular Culture*, 1976, vol. 9, pp. 878–85.

Kelly, A., '*All Quiet on the Western Front*: "brutal cutting, stupid censors and bigoted politicos" (1930–1984)', *Historical Journal of Film, Radio and Television*, 1989, vol. 9, pp. 135–50.

— 'The Brutality of Military Incompetence: *Paths of Glory* (1957)', *Historical Journal of Film, Radio and Television*, 1993, vol. 13, pp. 215–27.

— 'The United States and the Anti-War Cinema of the First World War: the case of *Ned Med Vaabnene/Lay Down Your Arms*', *Krieg und Literatur/War and Literature*, vol. 6, 1994, pp. 53–60.

Lourie, E., 'Grand Illusions', *American Film*, January–February 1985, vol. 10, pp. 29–34.

Lyons, T. J., 'Hollywood and World War I, 1914–1918', *Journal of Popular Film*, 1972, vol. 1, pp. 15–30.

Marquis, A. G., 'Words as Weapons: propaganda in Britain and Germany during the First World War', *Journal of Contemporary History*, 1978, vol. 13, pp. 467–98.

Merritt, R., 'D. W. Griffith Directs the Great War: the making of *Hearts of the World*', *Quarterly Review of Film Studies*, 1981, vol. 6, pp. 45–65.

Mitchell, G., 'Making *All Quiet on the Western Front*', *American Cinematographer*, vol. 66, September 1985, pp. 34-43.

Murdoch, B., 'Translating the Western Front', *Antiquarian Book Monthly Review*, vol. 28, 1991, pp. 452-60.

Peet, C., ' Hollywood at War 1915–1918', *Esquire*, September 1936, pp. 60, 109.

Reeves, N., 'The Power of Film Propaganda – Myth or Reality?', *Historical Journal of Film, Radio and Television*, 1993, vol. 13, pp. 181–201.

Richards, J., 'The Last Flight', *Focus on Film*, Summer 1975, vol. 21, pp. 59–60.

— 'The British Board of Film Censors and Content Control in the 1930s: images of Britain', *Historical Journal of Film, Radio and Television*, 1981, vol. 1, pp. 95–116.

— 'The British Board of Film Censors and Content Control in the 1930s: foreign affairs', *Historical Journal of Film, Radio and Television*, 1982, vol. 2, pp. 39–48.

Robertson, J. C., 'British Film Censorship Goes to War', *Historical Journal of Film, Radio and Television*, 1982, vol. 2, pp. 49–64.

Robinson, D., 'The Old Lie', *Sight and Sound*, Autumn 1962, pp. 201–4.

— 'Dawn (1928): Edith Cavell and Anglo-German relations', *Historical Journal of Film, Radio and Television*, 1984, vol. 4, pp. 15–28.

Seton, M., 'The British Cinema 1914', *Sight and Sound*, Autumn 1937, pp. 126–8.

Shand, J. D., 'Doves Among the Eagles: German pacifists and their government during World War I', *Journal of Contemporary History*, 1975, vol. 10, pp. 95–108.

Sherie, F., 'The Man who Wrote "Journey's End"', *Strand Magazine*, 1930, pp. 157–63.

Simmons, J., 'Film and International Politics: the banning of *All Quiet on the Western Front* in Germany and Austria, 1930–1931', *Historian*, 1989, vol. 52, pp. 40–60.

Smither, R., '"A Wonderful Idea of the Fighting": the question of fakes in *The Battle of the Somme*', *Historical Journal of Film, Radio and Television*, 1993, vol. 13, pp. 149–68.

Soderbergh, P. A., '*Aux Armes!*: The Rise of the Hollywood War Film, 1916–1930', *The South Atlantic Quarterly*, 65, 1964.

— 'On War and the Movies: a reappraisal', *The Centennial Review*, 1976, vol. 11, 405–18.

Somlo, J., 'The First Generation of the Cinema', *The Penguin Film Review*, London, Penguin Books, September 1948, pp. 55–60.

Strebel, E. G., 'French Social Cinema and the Popular Front', *Journal of Contemporary History*, 1977, vol. 12, pp. 499–519.

Suttner, B., 'How I wrote "Lay Down Your Arms"', *The Independent*, 1 February 1906.

Welch, D., 'The Proletarian Cinema and the Weimar Republic', *Historical Journal of Film, Radio and Television*, 1981, vol. 1, pp. 3–18.

Whitehall, R., 'Great Films of the Century – No. 5, *Westfront 1918*', *Films and Filming*, September 1960, pp. 12–14, 34.

— 'One … Two … Three? A Study of the War Film', *Films and Filming*, August 1964, pp. 7–12.

Index